SCIENTIFIC AMERICAN EXPLORES BIG IDEAS

The Unsung Heroes of STEM

The Editors of *Scientific American*

SCIENTIFIC AMERICAN | EDUCATIONAL PUBLISHING

New York

Published in 2027 by Scientific American Educational Publishing
in association with **The Rosen Publishing Group**
2544 Clinton Street, Buffalo NY 14224

Contains material from Scientific American®, a division of Springer Nature America, Inc., reprinted by permission, as well as original material from The Rosen Publishing Group®.

First Edition

Scientific American
Lisa Pallatroni: Project Editor

Rosen Publishing
Nicole Horning : Compiling Editor
Michael Moy: Senior Graphic Designer

Cataloging-in-Publication Data
Names: Scientific American, Inc.
Title: The unsung heroes of STEM / edited by the Scientific American Editors. Description: Buffalo, New York : Scientific American Educational Publishing, an imprint of Rosen Publishing, 2027. | Series: Scientific American explores big ideas | Includes glossary and index.
Identifiers: ISBN 9781538314708 (pbk.) | ISBN 9781538314715 (library bound) | ISBN 9781538314722 (ebook)
Subjects: LCSH: Discoveries in science–Juvenile literature. | Science–Juvenile literature. | Technological innovations–Juvenile literature. | Engineering–Juvenile literature. | Mathematics–Juvenile literature. | Women in mathematics–Juvenile literature.
Classification: LCC Q180.55.D57 U578 2027 | DDC 509–dc23

Manufactured in the United States of America
Websites listed were live at the time of publication.

Cover: Stokkete/Shutterstock.com

CPSIA Compliance Information: Batch # CS27SA.
For Further Information contact Rosen Publishing at 1-800-237-9932.

CONTENTS

INTRODUCTION

Behind every major scientific breakthrough or technological advancement, there are people whose names you may never hear. They're solving problems, making discoveries, and pushing innovation forward, often without recognition. In the science, technology, engineering, and mathematics (STEM) industries, many people work quietly, shaping the future in ways that impact everyday life.

Innovation doesn't happen all at once, and it doesn't come from just one person. It's the result of countless ideas, experiments, and collaborations built over time. Many researchers dedicate their work to improving systems, solving complex challenges, and expanding what we know, often without widespread attention. Their contributions may not always make headlines, but they play a critical role in advancing knowledge and creating new possibilities.

This book is a collection of articles that explore the work of these often-overlooked individuals and the impact they've had across STEM fields. In Diverse Heroes of STEM, you'll learn about the importance of diversity in STEM fields. Innovations in Science highlights breakthroughs that have changed how we understand the world. In Advances in Technology, you'll discover the tools and systems used every day and the creators behind them. Engineering Marvels focuses on the design and construction of structures and solutions that solve real-world problems. Finally, Mathematics explores the mathematical ideas and discoveries that have impacted our world.

By looking beyond the most well-known names, a fuller picture of innovation begins to take shape. One that recognizes the many voices, ideas, and efforts that continue to move STEM forward. These stories highlight the importance of persistence, creativity, and collaboration, showing that progress is often built by many people working toward a common goal over time.

Section 1: Diverse Heroes of STEM

Finding Yourself and Your Community when You Are Black in STEM

By Devin Williams

Antonio T. Baines knows what it's like to feel alone in the lab. He lived it while getting his doctorate. "I was in this Ph.D. pharmacology/toxicology graduate program, and there was nobody who looked like me when I first got there," he says.

At the time, Baines, who is African American, was studying at the University of Arizona. He entered his graduate program with a friend, who was also Black. "She was in the master's program," Baines says, "but we were the only two."

Now, as an associate professor and a cancer researcher in the Department of Biological and Biomedical Sciences at North Carolina Central University, he is working to change such situations. He mentors, he teaches, and he is a spokesperson and advocate for the next generation of students of color coming into the sciences.

"I think representation is so important–you need to see folks who look like you, no matter who you are, and others need to see that, too" Baines says. "If you don't ever see it, then, is it possible?"

This discussion is part of a speaker series hosted by the Black Employee Network at Springer Nature, the publisher of *Scientific American*. The series aims to highlight Black contributions to STEM (science, technology, engineering and mathematics) a history that has not been widely recognized. It will cover career paths, role models and mentorship, and diversity in STEM.

Mentorship and Sponsorship Are Crucial for Advancing Inclusion in STEM

By Marlene Stewart

Charlotte Owens spoke with the Springer Nature Black Employee Network about her career path in biomedicine. She is now a vice president at the pharmaceutical company Takeda and head of its R&D Center for Health Equity and Patient Affairs, as well as an adjunct assistant professor at Morehouse School of Medicine. She was previously therapeutic area lead for women's health at the pharmaceutical company AbbVie.

Owens is all too aware of the lack of Black representation in STEM (science, technology, engineering and mathematics) and is optimistic that we are moving in the right direction. "But we need to continue to work in tangible ways to make things better," she says. People from underrepresented groups appreciate diversity in the field, Owens says, yet she knows that unfortunately this has not been a "mainstream topic." She observes that "until recently, it was taboo to discuss [race] openly. There is still a lack of comfort for many on this subject–across all fields of STEM."

Owens emphasizes the importance of mentorship and says she appreciates the opportunities that have been presented to her by people who supported her career from the beginning. Not everyone in the field will give up their time and provide real opportunities and steps for others to climb, she adds, but "that's what my mentors and sponsors have done for me."

Owens encourages more people to extend themselves to help others pursue careers in STEM fields and have the same opportunities as people from better represented backgrounds and groups.

This discussion is part of a speaker series hosted by the Black Employee Network at Springer Nature, the publisher of *Scientific American*. The series aims to highlight Black contributions to

STEM—a history that has not been widely recognized. It will cover career paths, role models and mentorship, and diversity in STEM.

About the Author

Marlene Stewart is a senior business development manager for Springer Nature based in London, where she is responsible for an international client base. She is U.K. lead of the Springer Nature Black Employee Network and co-leader of the Black table talk program behind this speaker series.

How to Fix Science's Diversity Problem

By Benjamin Deen

Growing up in the world of academia, it was impossible to miss the issue of representation in my field. I just had to look around at the faces walking the halls of the elite institutions I was lucky to inhabit. I worked as an undergrad in Yale's psychology department, where one out of 31 current faculty members is Black. I did my Ph.D. in MIT's brain and cognitive sciences department, where one out of 57 professors was Black. I'm now a postdoc at Rockefeller University, where one out of 78 heads of lab is Black, and the first Black professor in the university's history, Erich Jarvis, didn't join the faculty until in 2016. These liberal strongholds, which have openly espoused the values of diversity and inclusion for decades, remain very white at the top levels.

A few weeks ago, our country watched George Floyd be slowly choked to death by a police officer, while pleading for his life. Amid the ensuing nationwide uprising against police brutality and systemic racism, a growing movement of academics has intensified its call to address discrimination and underrepresentation in science. The movement demands that all of us in the field pause and self-reflect: Are we doing all that we can to move the system toward a better outcome? Are we doing anything to perpetuate the status quo, even without noticing?

I come to these questions with a complicated background. I look like and culturally identify as a white person, but my heritage comprises an odd mix: I'm an eighth Black, a quarter Jewish, and otherwise a mix of German, Austrian, English and Irish. From a young age, I heard my dad's stories of being stared at or asked not to enter a beach because his mom was half Black. I have close cousins who are mostly Black and identify as such. Through my heritage and family, I feel attached to multiple historically oppressed groups. But when I interact with the NYPD, I have all the privilege of a white man. It's a curious feeling to know that I benefit from a system that actively oppresses my family members.

So, I enter the conversation on representation in academia with somewhat of a split identity–deeply empathizing with underrepresented groups, but also feeling some guilt about my own potential involvement. Through this lens, I've been interrogating myself, putting a microscope on my own behavior. I recently started a fellowship that involves a role in selecting speakers for Rockefeller's neuroscience seminar series, and had submitted a list of 17 young neuroscientists to invite. I wasn't actively thinking about race and representation when I made the list; I just thought briefly about whom I was excited to hear speak. On June 10, 2020, as calls to #ShutDownSTEM and #ShutDownAcademia encouraged scientists worldwide to consider these issues, I looked back at my list. I immediately noticed a familiar problem: 90 percent of the names were white professors.

It's one thing to hear slogans like "white silence is violence." It's another to directly observe the subtle mechanics of systemic discrimination, self-perpetuating through your own behavior.

I spent the next hour or so thinking about academics of color to add to this list. And I found that it wasn't hard to think of these people; it just wasn't my default. The next time I make a list of potential speakers for seminars or conference symposia, I won't forget to think about race.

As bothered as I was by my own behavior, I'm inspired by the simplicity of the fix: just flag the importance of representation when making decisions about who exists and is heard in academia. Scientists at all levels make these decisions. As trainees, we decide whom to cite in our manuscripts, whose research to read and engage with. Later, we begin choosing people to invite to talks, and students to mentor. Ultimately, as senior scientists, we have an even more direct gatekeeping role, deciding whom to hire and, thus, who constitutes the scientific enterprise. These choices are all levers that can be used to nudge the system away from its default, white male–heavy state.

We tend to think about racism as a personality trait: someone can be racist, nonracist or antiracist. But this simple model that we use to understand other people belies an incredibly complex underlying reality. We contain multitudes. We can be aware of the problems, read Baldwin and Coates, and still have patterns of thinking and behavior that perpetuate racial discrimination.

I'm not sure if we can convince the rest of the country to make concrete behavioral changes, to focus their effort on this issue and face the uncomfortable need to change. But I have more hope for science, which is largely composed of liberal and thoughtful people. The growing size of the movement against systemic racism in science shows that many academics are open and willing to evaluate the system that they and their behavior create. Effectively fighting deeply entrenched patterns of discriminatory behavior will require a widespread and sustained movement. If we can pull this off, maybe a future version of me will find neuroscience departments with more Black and brown faces.

About the Author

Benjamin Deen, Ph.D., is a postdoc in neuroscience at Rockefeller University.

Where Are the Black Women in STEM Leadership?

By Erika Jefferson

Today, Black women are working in every industry imaginable and doing jobs that, just a generation or two ago, we could only dream of. Yet the number of those working at senior levels in STEM fields remains distressingly low. In March, the National Science Foundation reported that in 2016 alone, Black women earned more than 33,000 bachelor's degrees in science and engineering, and 24 percent of doctorates awarded to Black women were in STEM. But that same report showed that in 2017, only 5 percent of managerial jobs in STEM were held by Black women and men combined. So, where are we?

This disparity is occurring amid record employment levels, and there is a critical need for qualified technical workers–but we cannot expect women and underrepresented minorities to remain in work environments where they cannot grow and thrive. We also cannot expect girls to enter fields where they do not see positive role models. It is imperative that we stop the constant drip from the leaky STEM pipeline by working hard to retain women–and especially underrepresented women of color–from the middle to the end.

Not only is this important for today's workforce needs, but also for tomorrow's. Despite our best efforts to encourage future generations to become scientists and engineers, there is no guarantee they will enter or stay in the STEM workforce once their education is complete. Without an influx of new talent each year, the United States will far further behind other nations in innovative and technological advances. Let's spend more time and money to ensure we can keep those Black women who are determined enough to make science a career.

At one time, Fortune 500 companies had their pick of the top graduates from the best schools, but no more. A brilliant young engineer from a top university will be heavily recruited but is just as likely to create her own company as go to work for a long-established one. Some industries are already feeling the impact of this and are trying to adapt. In the last several years, there have been some attempts to stem this rising tide by reaching out to a broader demographic of potential workers.

While leaders may say this is to address the ongoing gender imbalance in technical fields, dig a little deeper and it becomes clear companies already know they will not have enough capable talent to fill these roles in the digital revolution and are trying prepare for the loss of a preferred demographic.

Globally, we are still struggling to attract and retain women in STEM fields. While the problem has been getting more attention, the change is occurring much too slowly. The underlying reasons why diversity and inclusivity have not taken root have not changed over time. Women and minorities cite feelings of isolation, mistreatment by colleagues and management, and lack of opportunities for advancement as the reasons they leave STEM fields.

One solution is to create more diversity and inclusivity in emerging technologies by preparing underrepresented women already in STEM for roles in leadership. These efforts would provide the skills necessary for diverse women with traditional STEM degrees to rapidly transition into emerging technologies such as artificial intelligence, virtual reality, the Internet of Things and cybersecurity, while leveraging their previous experience and preparing them for leadership. Such resources could ensure women with technical backgrounds get the support necessary to become leaders in these industries far more quickly than we could by waiting on the next generation of workers to advance.

And more diverse leaders in these fields are needed for there to be a significant impact that creates the enduring change of including women and people of color in all areas of technology. It is critically important girls and women around the world have role models, mentors and champions in the workplace of the future who look like them. By training diverse women already in technical roles to become leaders, the entire ecosystem benefits. Women scientists and engineers understand the challenges of working in male-dominated fields and can better prepare others wanting to learn how to excel in management and entrepreneurship.

In 2015, we launched Black Women in Science and Engineering (BWISE) to support underrepresented women via networking, mentoring and career development. The group consists of women with degrees in science, technology, engineering and math, even if they no longer work in these areas. Research has shown diverse companies are more productive and successful. A dire shortage of STEM workers is predicted in the next 20 years, so it is imperative that young Black women be included in the workforce. Few companies have workforce affinity groups (associations based on shared experiences and backgrounds); these types of organizations are known to build support and morale among workers who feel acknowledged, valued and included within the larger corporate structure.

With BWISE, employees can get what they need despite—or in addition to—company offerings. Here, they have a safe space to discuss challenges and receive coaching, training and insight outside of the workplace. Companies can sponsor employees to be a part of BWISE to supplement their existing diversity efforts and can also assist by bringing in speakers and supporting our events. The organization helps to prepare, train and develop the next generation of Black women leaders in STEM.

We also have hosted successful networking events across the country in Atlanta, Austin, Chicago, Houston and Washington. Each event attracts the best and brightest in the STEM field, ranging from mid-career to top-level executives. In 2019, we will expand to three more cities—Boston, Dallas and New York—and provide more in-depth trainings in emerging technologies to meet the career demands of our membership.

The network of BWISE chapters and women around the world consists of experts and thought leaders in business, government and academia who are focused on engaging and empowering girls and women everywhere to join the digital revolution. Our members from the U.S., Europe and Africa are poised to become leaders in their own countries, impacting the lives of underrepresented people around the globe. By creating a more diverse workforce globally in emerging technology fields, we can help reduce gender-based financial inequities and be better prepared for the workplace of the future.

About the Author

Erika Jefferson is the President and Founder of Black Women in Science and Engineering (BWISE), an organization focused on bridging the leadership gap for Black women in STEM. She received her MBA from Georgia Tech and her BS in Chemical Engineering from LSU. She has worked for top companies such as Amoco, BP, Chevron and Praxair in a myriad of leadership roles ranging from sales/business development to supply chain and operations excellence.

The Time to Dismantle the Racial Structures That Pervade Global Science Is Now

By Devin Williams

"When you're dealing with an institutional structure like global science, one of its core features is that it has been a racial structure," says sociologist Anthony Ryan Hatch, an associate professor and chair of the Science in Society Program at Wesleyan University. "To dismantle and chip away at that system requires concerted effort, concerted resources, clear thinking, and a concern for equity and making things right."

But Hatch believes that even the effort to diversify institutions of higher learning, in terms of students and administration, has a potentially fraught set of challenges:

These structures are very resistant to change. And they are difficult to challenge, because in some cases, it involves directly not just calling out individual gatekeepers (key faculty members or deans or university heads or center heads) who are making biased decisions and who are letting assumptions about the excellence of, say, a candidate, the perceived excellence or lack thereof..., determine who gets a job–basically, just being racist. It's one thing to think about the individual people you might need to challenge, but when a structure produces these kinds of racial patterns, it's so much more challenging to intervene.

Hatch works and lives at the intersection of several fields: health, the environment, criminal justice and medicine. He says he was able to access that many disciplines through a combination of the "empathy and grace" he was shown as a student and a series of mentoring programs for students of color.

Those experiences helped Hatch navigate the predominately white institutions he was attending. "I never felt that I was cast out to sea–that I didn't have a support network to help me with my research, to help me improve my teaching, to help me pursue funding opportunities for my work," he says.

Hatch began his academic career in community-based public health research at Emory University, where he worked on projects related to drug use, HIV/AIDS and mental health. He is the author of *Silent Cells: The Secret Drugging of Captive America* and *Blood Sugar: Racial Pharmacology and Food Justice in Black America*. He has also held training fellowships at the American Sociological Association, the National Institute of Mental Health and the National Science Foundation, and was a faculty fellow at Wesleyan's Center for the Humanities.

Hatch knows that he was lucky. And he also knows that his success—and that of other researchers of color like him—does not mean that the work is done or that apparent progress is always true progress.

"I think that we're at a very interesting moment, and it's one that's filled with tension or contradiction," he says. "On one hand, you have a small class of well-trained scientists of color, and they have, through struggle and through sacrifice and through being positioned in the right networks..., risen to positions of power. And they're highly visible. And in their visibility, they become both target and object to be consumed."

Hatch says that to make real and lasting progress on diversity in science, one must look past that objectification. "One thing ... that is needed," he says, "is for people to have a good, clear-eyed sense of that distinction between the representation, the image of diversity—the image that we fixed the problem—and looking carefully at the structural reality."

Section 2: Innovations in Science

A 100-Year-Old Theory Might Explain What's Wrong with Quantum Mechanics

By Tim Folger

Quantum mechanics is both the most powerful theory physicists have ever devised and the most baffling. On the one hand, countless experiments have confirmed its predictions; the theory undergirds modern technology and enables the electronic devices we use every day. On the other hand, quantum mechanics describes an underlying reality that is utterly at odds with the world we perceive. In the quantum realm, a single particle exists in many places at once—at least while no one is looking at it. The theory also allows for inexplicable connectedness: a pair of atoms, no matter how widely separated, can be "entangled," such that whatever happens to one atom instantaneously affects the other. Albert Einstein called the phenomenon "spooky action at a distance."

These paradoxes have defined—or plagued—the theory since its inception more than a century ago. To this day, physicists still don't agree on what quantum mechanics is telling us about the nature of reality. Are there multiple universes? Do things come into existence only when they're observed? Is consciousness somehow central to the laws of physics? And what if all these mysteries could have been resolved right at the birth of quantum mechanics?

That's the case that Antony Valentini, a physicist at Imperial College London, makes in his new book *Beyond the Quantum: A Quest for the Origin and Hidden Meaning of Quantum Mechanics* (Oxford University Press, 2026).

Valentini argues that Louis de Broglie, a French physicist and Nobel laureate, developed a framework for quantum mechanics that eliminated its paradoxes around 100 years ago. In pilot wave theory, as de Broglie's brainchild is known, particles are guided by attendant waves. The particles themselves are always in one position and one position only; it is the spatially extended pilot wave that creates the impression that a particle is at once here and there. There's no need for an observer to conjure that particle into being. Even though de Broglie's conjecture in 1924 about the wavelike nature of matter was quickly confirmed by experiment and became integral to quantum theory, the physics community discounted or misrepresented the larger ideas from which he derived his key insights.

Valentini has spent his entire career championing and extending de Broglie's views. He recently spoke to *Scientific American* about his lonely path and why de Broglie might have been on to something.

[*An edited transcript of the interview follows.*]

In the history of science, has there ever been another situation like this, where there have been such wildly divergent views about what a theory means?

I'm not sure there has. If you go back to the time of [Isaac] Newton, he thought that space was empty and that there was a direct gravitational action at a distance. And on the continent, there were the Cartesians [followers of mathematician and philosopher René Descartes], who thought, "Oh no, space is full of this material medium, and that explains gravitational attraction." But [the debate] didn't last all that long. Certainly in the quantum case, the sheer variety of interpretations that say such completely different things about the world—I think it's a pretty safe bet that there's no analogue in the history of science.

One of the most striking things about modern physics is the stark divide between the macroscopic and quantum worlds, each of which seems to be governed by entirely different physical laws. You liken this to the way medieval astronomers split the cosmos into earthly and celestial regions.

I think it's a useful and valid parallel, this idea that there was a heavenly realm that we couldn't understand; anything above the moon and beyond was eternal and unchanging, completely different from the sublunar world, which was made of ordinary, imperfect matter that was always changing. It's a distinction that goes back to Aristotle. The parallel with quantum mechanics is extraordinary, that the quantum system is something that our mind can't understand. We can only understand the macroscopic one.

Austrian physicist Erwin Schrödinger developed quantum theory's wave equation, which describes quantum systems as waves that evolve with time. What role did this equation play in the so-called measurement problem: If a particle exists in different places at once, why do measurements find any given particle in only a single location?

Schrödinger created the measurement problem by removing the particles from de Broglie's theory. Mathematically, a [quantum wave] is a superposition of many different positions: a particle can be here and here and here; it can be anywhere. You can have a superposition of a live cat and a dead cat, or a superposition of different energies. They're all just different variations on the same theme. The wave equation contains all possible positions. How can you then explain that we see this little pointlike object if the only reality is an extended wave?

And this conundrum was recognized early in the development of quantum theory.

Here's Wolfgang Pauli writing to Niels Bohr in 1927: "In the last issue of the Journal de Physique, a paper by de Broglie has appeared.... It is very rich in ideas and very sharp, and on a much higher level than the childish papers by Schrödinger, who even today still thinks he may ... abolish material points." And because Schrödinger removed [particles from his equation], we've ended up with decades of confusion.

Why do you think de Broglie's theory was set aside and neglected?

I'm not sure there is one simple answer. It's maybe a mix of reasons.

In 1923 de Broglie had developed a new theory of motion. It was a complete break, very different from Newtonian or even Einsteinian physics. And yet this completely passed people by. The only thing that entered the collective consciousness of physicists was that de Broglie had shown that a particle can behave like a wave.

Word of de Broglie's thesis spread, though hardly anyone actually read it. Einstein did. It was Einstein who really alerted people that de Broglie had done something very important. He encouraged Schrödinger to read it–and he read it. Most other people, it seems, never read de Broglie's thesis.

And then there is the sociological point that de Broglie was quite isolated in Paris. De Broglie was a bit of a loner; he worked essentially by himself. At that time, in the 1920s, France was really a backwater in theoretical physics. It was strong in experimental physics, strong in mathematics but not in theoretical physics.

Has your pursuit of pilot wave theory been a lonely one? Rewarding? Frustrating?

The short answer is all of that and more. Has it been lonely? It's been this peculiar situation. I've really tried to get the key points across to physicists. And it just seems to fall on deaf ears. It's as if people are stuck on repeat–the same wrong arguments, the same historical misconceptions just go around and around and around.

When I first came across pilot wave theory, it seemed to me so obvious. Oh my god, pilot wave theory in principle is a wider physics; quantum theory is a special case of something bigger. Pilot wave theory has exciting new physics, and maybe we can find evidence for it.

In your book, you describe how pilot wave theory's predictions about the physics of matter differ in some cases from the predictions of accepted quantum mechanics. In particular, you mention how the cosmic microwave background (CMB)—the radiation created during the big bang that now permeates the universe—might support some of the predictions of pilot wave theory.

The CMB is an excellent and promising avenue, and I've done a lot of work on that with various collaborators. There are reported anomalies in the CMB that qualitatively match the kind of anomalies that pilot wave theory would predict. There are some tantalizing hints, but the data are just too noisy to draw any firm conclusions. This probably won't be settled for another 10 years or so.

Is pilot wave theory true? Is it an accurate theory of the world? If I knew it was true, I wouldn't be researching it. There's always, in the back of my mind, the thought that this could all be completely wrong! Or it could be that it's sort of partly right. In the late 19th century Ludwig Boltzmann modeled [gas molecules] as little billiard balls—little hard spheres that are bouncing around. It turns out that molecules are much more complicated than that. But still, his model contained a lot of truth. It might be that pilot wave theory is a bit like that, an approximate model.

About the Author

Tim Folger is a freelance journalist who writes for National Geographic, Discover, *and other national publications.*

Physicists Trace Particles Back to the Quantum Vacuum

By Clara Moskowitz

Quantum physics paints a strange picture of the world, one filled with spooky connections, unsettling uncertainties and—perhaps oddest of all—particles that spontaneously spring into being from the void. These so-called virtual particles have indirect effects that scientists have measured before. But now, for the first time, researchers have traced the evolution of these something-out-of-nothing particles directly.

In a study published today in Nature, physicists at the Relativistic Heavy Ion Collider (RHIC) at Long Island's Brookhaven National Laboratory describe how they found pairs of subatomic particles with an uncanny correlation in the direction of their spin. Particle spin is a quantum property that can point either up or down. Most groups of particles will have a random mix of up and down spins, but the researchers found that a particular kind of particle that has been produced at the collider has often come in pairs with matching spin directions.

These pairs, the scientists think, must be direct descendants of sets of virtual particles that spontaneously arose out of nothing from the quantum vacuum.

"The vacuum in quantum theory is not empty space," says physicist Dmitri Kharzeev of Stony Brook University. "It's a field filled with virtual particles." Such particles are a consequence of Heisenberg's uncertainty principle, which states that certain correlated properties—such as the energy and the lifetime of a quantum state—cannot both be known with precision. If a quantum state is very, very brief, then its energy can be highly uncertain. This means that pairs of particles—a particle and its antimatter partner—can briefly come into being by borrowing energy from nothing.

Usually these particles almost immediately disappear again by annihilating each other–but not this time.

Within RHIC, scientists smash protons together at nearly the speed of light to produce explosions of astounding energy. When a virtual particle pair happens to arise in the vacuum there, it can commandeer the freely available energy of the collision to become real. "When two particles collide at high energies, it gives the vacuum an energy boost," says Brookhaven physicist Zhoudunming (Kong) Tu, who was one of the authors of the new study. "Now the virtual particles get a push without having to annihilate back to the vacuum."

Using the Solenoidal Tracker at RHIC (STAR) detector, physicists were able to trace this process. The details of how they did so, though, might make your head spin.

Because these newly real particles originated as a pair, they are entangled, retaining a connection regardless of how far they may be separated. So when they fly apart after the collision, they share the same direction of spin.

The experiment traced pairs of "strange" quarks–cousins to the "up" and "down" quarks that make up protons and neutrons. Quarks aren't stable on their own, so when the new quarks sprang into existence, they quickly joined with others to form conglomerate particles called lambda hyperons. These are exotic versions of protons contain an up quark, a down quark and a strange quark instead of the proton's two ups and one down.

Lambdas, in turn, aren't so stable themselves. They last for only about 10–10 second and travel a few centimeters inside the collider before they decay into more mundane particles that STAR can see.

The direction of the momentum for these decay particles reveals the spin of the lambda hyperons that created them. And the spin of the lambda is thought to be determined solely by the spin of its strange quark (because the spins of its up and down quarks cancel out).

When the researchers looked at their measurements, they were surprised at how correlated these particles were. "Their spins seem to be parallel," says study co-author Jan Vanek, a physicist at the University of New Hampshire. "That hints we are actually seeing these vacuum strange quark pairs found in these lambda hyperons."

The finding confirms a 30-year-old prediction by Kharzeev and his colleagues that strange quark virtual particle pairs must have parallel spins. "It's exciting because you can come up with plausible theoretical ideas in your head, but you never know whether nature follows this or not," he says. "So to see that this was finally measured in a real experiment is very gratifying."

This new window on virtual particles should help answer a major mystery in nuclear physics: Where does a proton's mass come from? The three quarks that form protons only contribute a minuscule amount of mass–the other 99 percent is thought to arise from interactions between these real quarks and swarms of virtual quarks in the vacuum. "If we can trace a pair of quarks from virtual particle to real particle, maybe we can gain some insight about how this mass is generated through the interaction with the vacuum," Tu says.

The discovery also marks another achievement for RHIC as the collider prepares to shut down. Friday will be its last day of collisions, after a record-breaking 25-year-long run. Parts of the machine will be repurposed in Brookhaven's upcoming Electron-Ion Collider, which is set to start up at the lab in the mid-2030s.

About the Author

Clara Moskowitz is chief of reporters at Scientific American, *where she covers astronomy, space, physics and mathematics. She has been at* Scientific American *for more than a decade; previously she worked at Space.com. Moskowitz has reported live from rocket launches, space shuttle liftoffs and landings, suborbital spaceflight training, mountaintop observatories, and more. She has a bachelor's degree in astronomy and physics from Wesleyan University and a graduate degree in science communication from the University of California, Santa Cruz.*

A "Charmed" New Particle is Discovered at World's Largest Atom Smasher

By Clara Moskowitz

Physicists just discovered a brand-new particle that appears to be an exotic cousin to the protons and neutrons that make up atoms.

Those mundane subatomic particles are made up of even smaller building blocks of matter called "up" and "down" quarks, which are the lightest kinds of quarks. But quarks come in heavier flavors as well, including "charm," "strange," "bottom" and "top" (the most massive fundamental particle known).

The new particle, discovered at the world's largest atom smasher, the Large Hadron Collider (LHC) in Geneva, Switzerland, contains two charm quarks and a down quark. Like protons and neutrons, its total of three quarks classifies it in particle physics as a baryon, which is a type of hadron–or a particle made of quarks. The discovery brings the current tally of known hadrons discovered by LHC experiments to 80.

The new particle, which physicists are calling a doubly charmed baryon, essentially replaces the two up quarks in a proton with charm quarks, giving it about four times the mass of the more common and stable proton.

The LHC accelerates protons to more than 99 percent the speed of light and then slams them together. The protons are destroyed, and the energy of the crash gives rise to new particles in their wake. Every time a doubly charmed baryon was created within the collider, it quickly decayed into lighter particles.

The new particle was discovered by the LHCb experiment, one of nine detectors stationed around the LHC's 17-mile-long ring. It's the first new particle seen at the experiment since scientists upgraded LHCb in 2023.

The doubly charmed baryon is only the second baryon with two heavy quarks ever seen–the rest have all contained two up or down quarks and just one of the heavier flavors. The previous heavy baryon was discovered in 2017, also at LHCb, and consists of two charm quarks and an up quark. Despite their similarities, the newfound particle is even less stable than the other heavy baryon, with a lifetime predicted to be about six times shorter.

Finding these kinds of particles helps teach physicists about the strong force, which is the most powerful force in nature and binds hadrons together. The strong force is also the most mysterious and confusing force, governed by a complex theory called quantum chromodynamics. Physicists hope to understand how the strong force holds quarks together and how the composite particles' properties, such as mass and spin, arise.

Physicists announced the discovery this week at the Moriond particle physics conference in Italy.

About the Author

Clara Moskowitz is chief of reporters at Scientific American, *where she covers astronomy, space, physics and mathematics. She has been at* Scientific American *for more than a decade; previously she worked at Space.com. Moskowitz has reported live from rocket launches, space shuttle liftoffs and landings, suborbital spaceflight training, mountaintop observatories, and more. She has a bachelor's degree in astronomy and physics from Wesleyan University and a graduate degree in science communication from the University of California, Santa Cruz.*

What Is CRISPR, and Why Is It So Important?

By Michael Tabb, Andrea Gawrylewski & Jeffery DelViscio

CRISPR is the basis of a revolutionary gene editing system. One day, it could make it possible to do everything from resurrect extinct species to develop cures for chronic disease.

It's built on a natural adaptation found in the DNA of bacteria and single-celled organisms.

CRISPR stands for Clustered Regularly Interspaced Short Palindromic Repeats.

They're really just bits of genetic code with a specific, recognizable format. They contain a sequence that shows up over and over again, though it's often reversed each time.

That's what makes it "Palindromic:" palindromes are words that can be read the same backwards as forwards. Palindromes are common in DNA. Some serve as backups for damage to our genetic code, while others are common in cancer mutations.

With CRISPR, a group of enzymes recognize certain repeats, and break the DNA there to insert important information in the middle. These insertions are called "spacers," and they contain the genetic code of different viruses that have invaded in the past.

Such previous invasions served a very important evolutionary purpose: immunizing against foreign threats.

Researchers first discovered CRISPR in E. Coli in the 1980s. When E. coli survives viral attacks, it incorporates some of the virus DNA into its own genetic code.

E. Coli isn't unique in using this strategy. Between the 1980s and 2000, scientists found that lots of bacteria and single-celled organisms incorporate viral DNA this way.

Cells use these sequences as templates for transcribing complementary strands of RNA.

When viruses matching the template sequence enter the cell, the complementary RNA binds to them, and directs a series of CRISPR-associated enzymes, or "Cas" enzymes, to attack–cutting invader DNA at the binding site. That neutralizes the viral threat.

The CRISPR-Cas system is incredibly effective. It's also easy to manipulate, letting us alter a cell's genetic code however we want.

In 2012, French microbiologist Emmanuelle Charpentier and American biochemist Jennifer Doudna discovered that Cas enzymes–specifically Cas9–can be reprogrammed to cut nearly any part of the genome, using RNA sequences made in a lab. Those "guide RNA" molecules tell Cas9 where to cut DNA in a cell.

For their discovery, Charpentier and Doudna won the Nobel Prize in Chemistry in 2020.

And the use of CRISPR has taken off in science since their breakthrough.

But scientists are still far from realizing CRISPR's potential.

Cas9 is great at suppressing or knocking out unwanted genes. But for most medical purposes, it's not enough to cut unwanted DNA out. Scientists need to control how the DNA repairs itself.

Left to their own devices, cells tend to repair broken DNA using a method that introduces lots of random errors. Researchers can provide cells with templates to guide the repair process, but they're still working on making that more reliable.

Researchers have found lots of applications for CRISPR in animals, like making disease-resistant chickensand pigs, and mosquitos that can't bite or lay eggs. But they've got many projects underway, like making disease-resistant crops–including wine grapes. More ambitiously, they're working to genetically alter pigs so their organs could be transplanted into humans. And bring extinct species such as the passenger pigeon back to life, by tweaking the genomes of similar birds.

When it comes to the human genome, though, scientists have been more hesitant. Editing our own DNA could easily end up causing more problems than it solves.

While Cas9 reliably cuts DNA where we want it to, recent experiments have shown it can also affect genes far off-target. And even if we could get it to work reliably, many experts have flagged ethical concerns about using the technology for eugenics and "designer babies." If parents can one day pay scientists to edit their babies' DNA, making them stronger and smarter, CRISPR could make the world even more unequal and prejudiced.

In 2018, Chinese researcher HEH JEE'-an-qway claimed he'd used CRISPR to make HIV-resistant children. Whether or not he succeeded, his work violated China's National Health Commission rules, and he was sentenced to three years in prison.

Using CRISPR on babies is widely illegal. But there are some cases where using CRISPR on humans may be worth the risk.

In 2020, American researchers began the first clinical trials injecting CRISPR directly into living humans, aiming to repair a genetic mutation that causes blindness.

Many researchers hope CRISPR-based therapies could eventually cure hereditary diseases; they've already seen promising results in various animal studies. Though given the risks of editing the human genome, we're still a ways off from widespread use of CRISPR in medicine.

CRISPR has given science a tool to reliably tinker with the code of life. But the question remains: can we do so safely and ethically, while avoiding the unintended consequences of such power?

About the Authors

Andrea Gawrylewski is chief newsletter editor at Scientific American. *She writes the daily Today in Science newsletter and oversees all other newsletters at the magazine. In addition, she manages all special editions and in the past was the editor for* Scientific American Mind, Scientific American Space &

Physics and Scientific American Health & Medicine. *Gawrylewski got her start in journalism at the Scientist magazine, where she was a features writer and editor for "hot" research papers in the life sciences. She spent more than six years in educational publishing, editing books for higher education in biology, environmental science and nutrition. She holds a master's degree in earth science and a master's degree in journalism, both from Columbia University, home of the Pulitzer Prize.*

Jeffery DelViscio is currently chief multimedia editor/executive producer at Scientific American. *He is former director of multimedia at STAT, where he oversaw all visual, audio and interactive journalism. Before that he spent more than eight years at the New York Times, where he worked on five different desks across the paper. He holds dual master's degrees in journalism and in Earth and environmental sciences from Columbia University. He has worked onboard oceanographic research vessels and tracked money and politics in science from Washington, D.C. He was a Knight Science Journalism Fellow at the Massachusetts Institute of Technology in 2018. His work has won numerous awards, including two News and Documentary Emmy Awards.*

FDA Approves First CRISPR Gene Editing Treatment for Sickle Cell Disease

By Sara Reardon

CRISPR, the gene-editing technology that has revolutionized biological research, is finally available as a medical treatment with regulatory approval. On December 8 the U.S. Food and Drug Administration approved the first CRISPR treatment for sickle cell disease.

The treatment, called exa-cel and made by the companies Vertex and CRISPR Therapeutics, edits a gene involved in red blood cell shape and function. It appears to functionally cure the disease for at least one year. The FDA's decision makes the U.S. the second country to approve a CRISPR therapy, following exa-cel's approval for sickle cell disease in the U.K. in November.

Scientifically speaking, exa-cel is "an incredible asset to have," says Michael DeBaun, a hematologist at Vanderbilt University. But it is still early to say whether the treatment will be permanent and without side effects, he adds.

The FDA also approved another type of gene therapy for sickle cell disease today called lovo-cel, which is made by the company bluebird bio.

What is Sickle Cell Disease, and How Does the New CRISPR Therapy Work?

The CRISPR system used in exa-cel targets genes that produce hemoglobin, the protein that carries oxygen in blood cells. In a form of sickle cell disease called sickle cell anemia, mutations in a gene called *HBB* affect the protein's structure, causing it to twist normally round red blood cells into a curved sickle shape. These sickled cells clog blood vessels, leading to severe pain and fatigue.

In a related condition called beta-thalassemia, which sometimes occurs with sickle cell anemia, the body does not produce enough hemoglobin or red blood cells, resulting in symptoms caused by low blood oxygen levels. These symptoms include fatigue and growth problems in children.

Exa-cel directs an enzyme called Cas9 to a gene, called *BCL11A*, that typically prevents the body from making a form of hemoglobin found only in fetuses. Cas9 deactivates *BCL11A* in bone marrow stem cells, where red blood cells are made, by cutting its DNA, and the cells begin producing the fetal hemoglobin and creating red blood cells with a normal round shape. In the new therapy, physicians remove a person's own bone marrow stem cells, edit them with exa-cel, destroy the rest of the person's untreated bone marrow and then reinfuse the edited cells.

Because these edited cells eventually repopulate the body, exa-cel is considered a "curative" therapy that will theoretically last the rest of the recipient's life, although Vertex and CRISPR Therapeutics have followed most of their trial participants for less than two years.

How Effective is the Treatment?

So far exa-cel has only been tested in around 100 people with either sickle cell anemia or beta-thalassemia. Nevertheless, in 2019 the FDA gave the companies a "fast-track" approval that allows it to test the therapy in smaller groups of people than would normally be required.

In these trials, which are still ongoing, 29 of the 30 study participants with sickle cell anemia had no pain for one year in the 18 months following their exa-cel transfusions. And 39 out of 42 beta-thalassemia patients no longer needed blood or bone marrow transplants–the standard treatment for this disease–for one year after the exa-cel intervention. Vertex and CRISPR Therapeutics are continuing to track the remaining participants who have not yet reached this time point and will follow all participants for up to 15 years.

What Are the Risks?

The results submitted to the FDA suggest that exa-cel has no major adverse health impacts, although it can cause side effects such as nausea and fever. But DeBaun points out that the participants have only been tracked for a short time and that problems could arise later.

Another concern raised by the FDA is that the Cas9 enzyme could remain active and cut the genome in places other than *BCL11A*, creating so-called off-target mutations. The companies modeled the most likely places in the genome where the enzyme could cut and found no evidence that this had happened in trial participants. "In light of any new therapy, we remain cautiously optimistic," DeBaun says.

Besides Exa-cel, What Are Some Other Promising Therapies for Sickle Cell Disease?

Bluebird bio's lovo-cel, the other gene therapy that was approved today by the FDA, uses a viral vector to deliver a functional version of an adult hemoglobin-producing gene and insert it permanently into a person's genome. The data bluebird bio submitted to the FDA showed lovo-cel was effective in 36 people who were followed for a median of 32 months. Dozens of studies are investigating other types of gene therapies for sickle cell anemia and beta-thalassemia that deliver normal versions of *HBB* or other genes to the body.

Researchers have found that a technique called haploidentical transplant could also cure sickle cell anemia. In this treatment, which is already widely used to treat certain cancers, a person's bone marrow cells are replaced with those from a parent or sibling who is 50 percent genetically identical to the recipient but does not have the disease. Results that will be presented next week at the American Society for Hematology's annual conference found that 88 percent of adults who received these transplants continued to make normal red blood cells after two years. DeBaun says this technique could be particularly useful in low- and middle-income countries because it is likely to cost much less than gene editing or gene therapy.

Will Exa-cel or Lovo-cell be Available to Everyone with Sickle Cell Disease?

Like most gene editing therapies, exa-cel and lovo-cell are likely to be very expensive. Neither Vertex, CRISPR Therapeutics nor bluebird bio have said how much their respective therapies will cost, but estimates suggest that the price for each could be as much as $2 million per patient. It is still unclear whether insurers, especially government services such as Medicaid, will cover the therapies or in which cases they will do so. Sickle cell disease disproportionately affects people of African descent, including African Americans, who are more likely to have public insurance through Medicaid than most other groups in the U.S.

DeBaun says that deciding whether to pursue CRISPR gene editing or another approach such as haploidentical transplant will need to be a shared decision by patients, their families and their physicians. Even if gene editing proves to be more effective at permanently curing the disease, it is likely to be less widely available and may take longer than a transplant from a donor.

Nevertheless, DeBaun says that exa-cel is a good first step, and he expects that the technology will improve as more is learned about CRISPR therapies over the next decade. "This is the first mile of a marathon," he says.

About the Author

Sara Reardon is a freelance biomedical journalist based in Bozeman, Mont. She is a former staff reporter at Nature, New Scientist and Science and has a master's degree in molecular biology.

What Does the First Pig-to-Human Lung Transplant Mean for Xenotransplantation?

By Humberto Basilio

Scientists announced this week that they have managed to keep a genetically modified pig lung alive inside a human body—although briefly—for the first time. The lung survived for nine days, marking what some researchers say is an early step toward a major, long-hoped-for medical breakthrough. But others note that the road ahead is still a lengthy one.

With available human organs constantly filling only a tiny fraction of transplant demand, scientists have been trying for decades to turn pigs into lifesaving donors. Many pig organs are close in size and structure to those of humans, and pigs are prolific breeders that are relatively easy to raise in a pathogen-free environment. Researchers have successfully transplanted pig kidneys, livers and hearts into humans, but lungs have remained a daunting challenge because of their complex physiology.

For one thing, lungs contain many blood vessels and white blood cells called macrophages, which surround and kill bacteria and viruses. These cells rapidly produce immune responses—but they also tend to trigger rapid and potentially lethal inflammation when surgeons restore blood flow after reducing it during transplant surgery. Because of such complexity, "we knew lungs would be the last organ that will get into the clinic," says Muhammad Mohiuddin, a surgeon and president of the International Xenotransplantation Association, who conducted the first pig-to-human heart transplantation in 2022 but was not involved with the new experiment. And although it "is a great achievement" for the field, "we have to be cautiously optimistic" because this is just an early foray into understanding this extremely difficult procedure.

A team of scientists at China's Guangzhou Medical University transplanted the pig lung into the body of a 39-year-old recipient who had already been declared brain-dead. The researchers used the gene-editing technique CRISPR to alter three pig genes that are naturally targeted by human antibodies. They also added three human genes to help prevent rejection. From the resulting genetically modified pig, they transplanted the left lung into the recipient, whose body was kept on life support, to observe how the organ functioned and how the human immune system responded. They also administered immunosuppressants to help prevent rejection.

The transplanted lung remained functional for nine days and was not immediately rejected by the human body. The scientists did report signs of lung tissue damage–produced by the lack of oxygen during the transplantation–one day after surgery, however. And the immune system showed the first signs of antibody-mediated rejection on days three and six. The experiment was terminated on day nine at the request of the recipient's family.

In the study, which was published in *Nature Medicine* this week, the authors said that the process needs significant improvements, such as optimizing the pig's genetic modifications and the immunosuppressive drugs used to avoid long-term rejection of the organ. None of the authors responded to *Scientific American*'s interview requests.

"I don't think blindly adding more knockouts and transgenes is the solution," says Columbia University immunologist Megan Sykes, referring to genetic changes to the donor pig. If scientists take that approach, she adds, each modification should be tested separately by transplanting the pig organs into a baboon–a primate that is often used as a prehuman test stop for transplants. Sykes was not involved with the surgery and has focused on pig-to-baboon experiments to establish a recipient's tolerance of transplanted lungs "I think tolerance, as well as better control of innate immunity, is going to be essential for the success," she says.

"It would have been nice to see if the lung was able to support life," says surgeon Richard Pierson of Harvard Medical School, who has also transplanted pig lungs into nonhuman primates. To test this ability, Pierson says, surgeons can block blood flow to a recipient's existing lung, leaving the transplanted lung to function by itself.

The longest a pig lung has survived after being transplanted into a baboon is 31 days. Pierson, who performed that surgery, says the new one–along with the clinically successful pig kidney transplants–"elicits enthusiasm" in the transplant medicine community. "It reminds us that there's real progress being made," he says.

Recent relaxations of countries' regulatory frameworks has expanded surgeons' opportunities to experiment with pig-to-human surgeries, making it likely that more such procedures will be attempted in the coming years, Mohiuddin says.

Pig kidney transplants in humans have shown successful results in recent years; these organs have functioned relatively well. Two people are currently living with a pig kidney–one in China who had the surgery in March and another in the U.S. who has had the new organ since January.

The latest preliminary surgery in a recipient with brain death cannot reveal much about the lung's long-term function, Mohiuddin says. But he adds that it can help scientists test immunosuppressive drugs that do not work the same way in baboon bodies.

Some difficult first steps are needed to advance the development of pig-to-human transplant surgeries that could one day save thousands of lives, according to Mohiuddin. He says he believed in the possibility of making a pig-to-human heart transplantation for decades before he could perform the surgery. "The progress will be slow," he adds, "but every advance that happens in this field is very critical."

About the Author

Humberto Basilio is a Mexican science journalist covering policy, health, misconduct, archaeology and the environment. He is also a former news intern at Scientific American. *His work has been published in the* New York Times, National Geographic, Science, Nature, *and more.*

Diagnosing Type 1 Diabetes before Symptoms Strike

By Rachel Nuwer

In 2024 Stephen Rich and his colleagues published a study in which they assessed the genetic risk of developing type 1 diabetes for more than 3,800 children from across Virginia. Almost immediately Rich, a genetic epidemiologist at the University of Virginia, was inundated by e-mails and calls from parents who had read the article and wanted their kids tested, too. Unfortunately the study was over, so Rich couldn't help them. But the experience exemplified the growing interest in genetic risk tests for the disease, he says.

There is currently no cure for type 1 diabetes, a chronic condition in which the body's immune system attacks and kills insulin-producing beta cells in the pancreas. Knowing someone's genetic predisposition to type 1 diabetes, however, can help doctors identify whom to flag for follow-up tests. It can also lead to earlier adoption of therapeutics to manage the disease or delay its onset. "There's tremendous power in terms of understanding the genetics of type 1 diabetes," says Todd Brusko, director of the Diabetes Institute at the University of Florida. As more therapies become available, he adds, the eventual hope is to use genetic profiling to determine who will respond best to one drug versus another.

Recent advances in genetic screening tools have not only revealed an intricate interaction between a person's genes and their immune system but also made it possible to imagine a future in which every newborn is screened for type 1 diabetes risk. Some health-care authorities are already beginning to consider universal screening. "It's very exciting times," says Maria Jose Redondo, a physician and professor of pediatric diabetes and endocrinology at the Baylor College of Medicine. "A lot of progress has been made, and now we're at the point of applying it."

In the U.S., around one in 300 people develops type 1 diabetes. Although the disease is best known for manifesting in children, adults account for almost half of new diagnoses. Scientists still don't know what triggers it. Environmental factors seem to play a crucial role in promoting the disease's development and progression, but the exact causative agents are unknown. "We know less about the environmental factors than we know about the genetic factors," Redondo says.

In a large study called TEDDY (for "the environmental determinants of diabetes in the young"), launched in 2004 in Europe and the U.S., researchers followed 8,676 individuals with high genetic risk to try to identify triggers for type 1 diabetes. They found just one consistent environmental factor linked to higher likelihood of acquiring the disease: early infection with enteroviruses, a type of virus that can infect beta cells. Not all children who get these common infections go on to develop type 1 diabetes, though, so additional factors are probably at play. In addition, the incidence of the disease has been increasing steadily over the past 60 years, suggesting that some change in environmental exposures or the removal of protective factors–or both–may be involved.

Genetics accounts for about half of a person's risk of developing the disease, meaning what is written into someone's DNA is "not destiny," Rich says. "If you have a high [genetic] risk, it doesn't mean you'll get it, and if you have a not-high risk, that doesn't mean you're protected."

For people with a close relative with type 1 diabetes, the risk goes up to about 18 in 300. Those with an identical twin with the disease have the highest risk–about one in two. They are 150 times likelier to develop the illness than someone with no family history and eight times likelier than someone with a parent or sibling who has been diagnosed. Even so, around 90 percent of people who are diagnosed with type 1 diabetes have no relatives with the disease. Until recently, population-level genetic screening, which would include individuals regardless of their known risk factors for the condition, was not a practical option. But new breakthroughs have begun to change that.

Scientists have identified at least 90 regions in the human genome that hold genes connected to type 1 diabetes. Researchers are most interested in a gene cluster called the human leukocyte antigen system (HLA), which encodes proteins that help the immune system distinguish self from nonself. This gene group accounts for around half of a person's genetic risk of developing the disease. Because it helps to protect us from infections, HLA is also highly variable, says Mark Anderson, director of the Diabetes Center at the University of California, San Francisco. "There's selective pressure for us to have different HLA genes because that way, a virus or bacterium that comes along won't wipe everyone out."

Most people who acquire type 1 diabetes have at least one of two specific-risk-conferring gene variants, or alleles, in this region. "This region is so critically important to whether we're susceptible to autoimmune diseases that just by measuring variation there, we can capture risk," says Richard Oram, a professor of diabetes and nephrology at the University of Exeter in England. Some HLA variants increase risk up to 20-fold, he adds, whereas others decrease risk by the same amount. In effect, it's as if 10 to 15 percent of people with European ancestry carried a genetic vaccine to type 1 diabetes, Oram says, referring to the HLA gene alleles that decrease risk.

In 2015 Oram and his colleagues developed the first version of what is now one of the most widely used tests for type 1 diabetes genetic risk, administered primarily in research settings (the U.S. has yet to approve any test for type 1 diabetes risk for real-world use in doctor offices). Rather than just adding up the contribution of each variant, Oram and his colleagues' test incorporates the complex interactivity of various alleles with one another, including ones with protective effects. They also incorporated dozens of other non-HLA sites—mostly from genes also related to the immune system—that contribute small amounts of individual risk but can add up to larger cumulative risk.

The original version of the test examined just 10 alleles and "worked pretty well," Oram says. The latest version, developed in 2019, uses 67 alleles and produces "highly sophisticated" results, Redondo says, adding that it now represents "the golden standard to date."

When Oram originally developed his test, he did not have risk prediction in mind; rather he was trying to decipher the type of diabetes in a group of his patients. The individuals he was working with, who were 20 to 40 years old, had overlapping features of type 1 and type 2 diabetes. People who fall into this "gray area" of symptoms are commonly misdiagnosed, he says. While brainstorming solutions over coffee with a colleague, Oram realized a genetic test could offer clues for people with a less clear presentation of the disease.

After successfully developing the test, Oram learned that other research groups were interested in tests to determine genetic risk for type 1 diabetes. Fortunately his test "also turned out to be really good for that," he says.

With Oram's test, doctors can identify the highest-risk individuals, who can then get tested for the antibodies that attack the body's beta cells. "If you do HLA screening followed by antibody testing at specific ages, you'll pick up far and away the vast majority of cases," says William Hagopian, a research professor of pediatrics at the Indiana University School of Medicine. Investigators leading vaccine and pharmaceutical trials for type 1 diabetes are also using genetic tests to maximize efficiency and funding by identifying participants who are most likely at risk for the disease.

Genetic risk scores can also help doctors identify people who should be prescribed teplizumab, the first therapy able to delay the onset of an autoimmune condition. Approved by the U.S. Food and Drug Administration in 2022, this monoclonal antibody is given before the body becomes dependent on insulin, and it can delay more severe illness by two to three years. "The whole field has changed because now we have something we can do to delay progression to clinical diabetes," says Kevan Herold, an immunologist and endocrinologist at Yale University. "Any time without diabetes is a gift, particularly for children and their families." Other drugs are in various stages of clinical testing.

People aware of their risk might also be on the lookout for symptoms such as excessive urination and lethargy; when those pop up, people can seek treatment before they develop diabetic ketoacidosis (DKA), a potentially life-threatening condition caused by a lack of insulin. Among those who don't know they are at risk, about 40 percent wind up in this critical state, but that number drops as low as 4 percent for those who are aware. "If people can identify some of the symptoms of progression toward disease, they could go to a GP instead of an ER and prevent a real crisis," Brusko says.

There is some evidence to support these benefits, based on outcomes from one of the largest testing efforts to date, launched in 2020 by investigators at Sanford Health, a nonprofit health-care system based in Sioux Falls, S.D. As of July 2025, the study had enrolled more than 13,000 children for genetic risk testing and antibody screening for type 1 diabetes and celiac disease. Children with persistent positive antibodies are offered ongoing monitoring. Of the 75-plus children in monitoring, five have progressed to hyperglycemia, warranting clinical care, and none of these children developed DKA. Kurt Griffin, principal investigator of the study and a pediatric endocrinologist at the Benaroya Research Institute in Seattle, says the findings have already demonstrated that it is feasible to integrate type 1 diabetes screening into routine pediatric care.

Type 1 diabetes has been most prevalent among people of European ancestry. It does occur in those of African, Hispanic and Asian ancestry, but the vast majority of data used to inform genetic screening results is from people of white, European descent, Rich says. This lack of representation is problematic for people of different ancestries because genetic risk factors differ across populations.

In an unpublished study, Rich and his colleagues tested how well the most common HLA variants used in genetic tests predicted risk in people with European, Hispanic, African American or Finnish ancestry. They found that genetic ancestry for important HLA regions—and the many other regions of the genome associated with type 1 diabetes risk—does not transfer well from one population to another. "One of the biggest needs in the field is to understand what confers genetic risk in a much more diverse genetic ancestry," Brusko says.

Scientists are working to fill this gap. For instance, Breakthrough T1D, a nonprofit organization funding research on type 1 diabetes, provides grants of up to $900,000 for research aimed at improving the prediction power of genetic risk scores across diverse populations. For the next version of the genetic risk score test, the plan is to incorporate specific HLA types present in Africans, East Asians, and several other groups, says Hagopian, who collaborates with Oram.

Genetic risk tests for type 1 diabetes are inching closer to use in clinical care. Last year Randox, a company based in Northern Ireland, released one developed with Oram and his colleagues. Commercial tests are not available yet in the U.S., but they are becoming more affordable for researchers who use them in laboratory-based settings. This affordability will translate to clinical settings once tests make their way to doctor offices. "The price has dropped and is predicted to drop even more," Redondo says. Now the biggest remaining obstacles are political and logistical rather than scientific or financial, experts say. "All the tools are there; we just haven't quite got countries over the line to figure out how they're going to do it," says Colin Dayan, a professor of clinical diabetes and metabolism at Cardiff University in Wales.

Europe has been at the forefront of these efforts, Brusko says. In 2023 Italy became the first nation to pass a law mandating type 1 diabetes genetic screening across its population, but it has yet to implement this screening in practice, Dayan says. Other countries, including the U.K., are debating whether they should do the same. This past June the U.K. also announced plans to sequence the genomes of all babies within the next decade. The data obtained could be used for risk screening as well, says Emily K. Sims, a pediatric endocrinologist at the Indiana University School of Medicine. In the U.S., genetic screening for type 1 diabetes is still done primarily in research environments. "We really need federal and state authorities to decide that this testing is worth it and that they want to adopt it into general practice," Hagopian says. The easiest way to implement such a program would be to screen at birth.

What to do with the information that testing would generate, though, is a more complicated question. Health-care officials would have to set up a system for contacting the families of babies at high risk to appropriately communicate the results. There would also need to be a system to remind families to get their child checked for autoantibodies at certain intervals. States handle newborn screenings differently, so each would have to come up with its own solutions. This issue is "a major complication that has to be figured out," says Rich, who continues to field e-mails and calls from parents interested in the testing.

As the science is refined, more treatment options will be made available, and the uncertainty surrounding who will and will not go on to develop type 1 diabetes is likely to be narrowed. Redondo and her colleagues are pursuing a large project using genetic risk scores and other variables to try to more accurately predict disease development. They are also working on models to determine who will respond best to new disease-modifying therapies. As Redondo says, "personalizing prevention of type 1 diabetes is the goal."

About the Author

Rachel Nuwer is a science journalist and author. Her latest book is I Feel Love: MDMA and the Quest for Connection in a Fractured World *(Bloomsbury, 2023). Follow her on Bluesky @rachelnuwer.bsky.social*

Cell Transplant Therapy Offers New Hope for Type 1 Diabetes

By Carin Leong

Carin Leong: What if people with type 1 diabetes could start making their own insulin?

Scientists have just taken a big step in that direction. They treated a patient with 80 million lab-made insulin-producing cells that are designed to hide from the immune system. This is the first time a cell transplant like this hasn't triggered a rejection in a human, and researchers say that this opens exciting possibilities for treating diabetes and other autoimmune diseases in the future.

About two million people in the U.S. currently live with type 1 diabetes. It's an autoimmune disease where the body mistakenly wipes out the cells in the pancreas that make insulin. Without this hormone, people have to rely on injections and pumps every single day to keep their blood sugar in check and avoid serious complications.

Scientists have tried replacing these insulin-producing cells before, but the body kept attacking them. And patients would need to take strong immune-suppressing drugs for life, which come with their own laundry list of side effects.

This time, researchers took donor cells and used the gene-editing technique CRISPR to deactivate two genes that normally flag the immune system to attack foreign cells while also boosting expression of a gene that discourages attacks by the body's immune cells.

So 12 weeks after injecting these cells into the patient, they were still alive and making insulin in his body. Granted, it wasn't a ton–about 7 percent of what he'd need to ditch insulin injections entirely. But experts say it's a major milestone for his body to be producing even a little bit of insulin on its own and, most importantly, without the need for immunosuppressants. They'll continue monitoring him over the next year and test higher doses of these edited cells. And if all goes well, this could potentially lead us toward a cure for type 1 diabetes.

About the Author

Carin Leong is a documentary filmmaker based in New York. Her projects have received support from Field of Vision, the Singapore International Film Festival, IN-DOCS, and the Tribeca Film Institute. Her work has appeared in Scientific American, Hakai Magazine, *and* The Atlantic. *She holds a master's degree in science journalism from Columbia University's Graduate School of Journalism and is also a graduate of New York University's Tisch School of the Arts.*

Genetic Discoveries Could Reduce Black Women's Higher Breast Cancer Death Risk

By Leah Small

Black women in the U.S. are close to 40 percent more likely to die of breast cancer than white women and twice as likely to be diagnosed with breast cancer before the age of 40.

The disparity adds to an alarming trend of women increasingly being diagnosed with breast cancer in early adulthood and middle age overall, the 2025 American Cancer Society's annual cancer report shows.

Health and income inequalities factor into why Black women die from breast cancer at disproportionate rates. But genetics also plays a significant role. In recent years, more researchers have joined a huge push to investigate genetic mysteries behind why Black women are more likely than any other racial group to die of breast cancer, have more aggressive tumors and develop breast cancer at a younger age—despite having a slightly lower overall incidence of breast cancer than white women.

More than 86 percent of DNA samples in genomics studies are from participants with European ancestry, and from 2016 to 2021, the proportion of samples from nonwhite populations either stayed the same or decreased. Human beings are 99.9 percent genetically identical, but their small degree of difference from one another has outsize implications for cancer and other diseases.

Certain genetic variants, or mutations, are often linked to ancestry, and some have been connected to poor health outcomes. Inherited variants in genes that keep inflammation and cell division in check can greatly influence cancer risk. For example, variants that turn off the *BRCA1* and *BRCA2* tumor suppressor genes are connected to a greater incidence of breast cancer in women of Ashkenazi Jewish descent.

In contrast, little is known about genetic variants that influence cancer risk for Black women because of decades of underrepresentation in genomic studies and clinical trials, says Melissa Davis, a Morehouse School of Medicine geneticist who leads one of the largest international collaborations on breast cancer disparities research.

"The groups of people who have been studied to identify genetic risk markers have largely been people of European descent," Davis says. "That means that genetic risk that exists in other groups has gone unnoticed–undocumented–but we know it exists."

Researchers are now including more people with African ancestry in genomic studies and have identified more variants that could impact breast cancer survivorship in Black women. And scientists are partnering internationally to share data, DNA repositories and other resources, which is leading to more discoveries that could improve cancer treatment for this population.

Why Breast Cancer Is More Deadly in Black Women

Deaths from breast cancer have been declining for all groups except Native American women since 1990–but the survival gap has widened between Black and white women.

More widespread use of mammograms, along with the implementation of targeted hormone therapies more than 40 years ago, has significantly contributed to the decline in death rates. But even though Black women are slightly more likely than white women to receive regular mammograms, targeted hormone therapies are often less effective for Black women.

"Prior to the mid-1980s, it didn't really matter whether you were Black or white, you pretty much had the same chance of surviving breast cancer," Davis says.

She and other scientists looked toward genetics to partly explain the difference in Black women's response to hormone therapy and the reasons they develop cancer younger and have more aggressive tumors.

In the early 2000s scientists noted the most aggressive tumors lacked the three receptors that respond to hormone therapies and termed this cancer subtype triple-negative breast cancer (TNBC). Black women are twice as likely as white women to develop this type of cancer—a major contributor to the mortality disparity. Davis was one of the earliest researchers to work on uncovering the genetic mechanisms behind triple-negative breast cancer.

"We started asking the question, 'What do these patients have in common that white women wouldn't have?'" Davis says. "That pointed directly to African ancestry."

Davis is former scientific director of the International Center for the Study of Breast Cancer Subtypes, one of the first large-scale international research cohorts to study breast cancer genetic disparities in women with African ancestry. She and the center's founder, Lisa Newman, a researcher and chief breast surgeon at Weill Cornell Medicine, were among the first researchers to observe that most TNBC cases globally occur in sub-Saharan West Africa. Most African Americans have sub-Saharan West African ancestry.

Working with institutions in Ghana and Ethiopia, Davis and Newman created a more inclusive picture of the human genome by mapping genetic profiles of people with African ancestry who have TNBC using tissue donated by African Americans and Africans.

Research by Davis has found that African American women were far more likely than white women to have an aggressive, androgen-receptor-negative subtype of TNBC. And a 2022 study co-authored by Davis showed that having a greater amount of quantifiable African ancestry—a DNA measurement independent of self-reported race—was linked with a larger number of immune cells in the tumors of Black women with TNBC. But these cancer-fighting cells were inactivated.

The discovery could inform the development of TNBC immunotherapies that may be more effective for Black women, who currently lack therapeutics personalized to their tumor characteristics, Davis and her Morehouse School of Medicine colleague Rachel Martini write. "The advent of every new technology or treatment protocol has propagated disparities in minoritized populations," they added.

Tracing Genetic Risks

Scientists have discovered cancer-linked gene variants unique to people of African ancestry, including one that confers protection against malaria.

Davis and other researchers have found that a variant in a gene called *DARC*—which controls inflammation, a key driver of cancer—causes the gene to be expressed at lower levels in people with sub-Saharan West African ancestry. *DARC* is expressed in red blood cells and tumors. In red blood cells, *DARC* produces a protein that malarial parasites can invade.

Low *DARC* expression in people with sub-Saharan West African ancestry evolved selectively because malaria is endemic in the region. But there is a disadvantage—lower levels of *DARC* in tumors are tied to reduced cancer survivorship.bDavis filed a patent for a test to measure *DARC* expression, which, if developed, could help determine cancer treatment plans for Black women.

In addition to *DARC*, researchers are also exploring how variants in the *BRCA1* and *BRCA2* tumor suppressor genes—which have been more widely studied in other groups—impact Black women. Multiple variants in the *BRCA1* and *BRCA2* tumor suppressor genes were found to be prevalent in Black women with breast cancer in Florida, according to a 2015 study conducted by researchers at the University of Florida study. The study's authors suggested that it may be beneficial for Black women who develop breast cancer at age 50 or younger to undergo *BRCA* screening.

And researchers at the African Ancestry Breast Cancer Genetic Consortium, led by Vanderbilt University Medical Center, published findings last May from what they say is possibly the largest genome-wide association study of women with African ancestry for breast cancer. The study, which included data from more than 40,000 women from several African countries, Barbados and the U.S., identified 12 variants associated with breast cancer in women with African ancestry. Three were tied to TNBC.

Progressive research practices–such as establishing larger research cohorts and sharing more data, as has been required by the National Institutes of Health–have been increasing the pace of genetic research on breast cancer disparities, says Brittany Jenkins-Lord, a molecular biologist at the Johns Hopkins Bloomberg School of Public Health.

"All of the [NIH-funded] studies are supposed to be FAIR [findable, accessible, interoperable and reusable]," Jenkins-Lord says. "In the past, you had to contact investigators yourself and ask them for the data," she adds. "They could decide whether or not they wanted to give it to you, and if you're a competitor, they might not."

Discovering more genetic variants also helps Black women assess their individual cancer risk, says Altovise Ewing-Crawford, a health equity geneticist at Genentech. Physicians are less likely to recommend Black patients for genetic testing because of a perceived lack of information about variants unique to African ancestry. Ewing-Crawford advises Black women to undergo genetic testing because of known variants–and because scientists are continually finding more.

"As genomic research becomes more inclusive and prioritizes the discovery of genetic variants in ... diverse populations, we may see the benefits of genetic testing extend more equitably," Ewing-Crawford says.

Other Cancer Risk Factors

Researchers are starting to understand how genetics interact with nonmedical health factors, such as institutional racism and environmental risks, to contribute to breast cancer death risk. "Making connections between environmental exposures and cancer has been done for probably a century now," Jenkins-Lord told the author of this article in an interview for a piece in *Hopkins Bloomberg Public Health* magazine. "You have your risk, you have your outcome, but in the middle, you have everything biological that's happening."

Jenkins-Lord and other researchers are studying the epigenetics of inner-city populations–ideal subjects because of their diversity of income and race–for additional insights. In Baltimore, where Jenkins-Lord works, the city's mostly white and affluent Cheswolde and Crosscountry neighborhoods have a 16-year-longer life expectancy than parts of the mostly Black neighborhoods Upton and Druid Heights, a divide related in part to cancer outcomes.

In Black women who lived in disadvantaged neighborhoods in Baltimore, Jenkins-Lord found that a key tumor suppressor gene was expressed at lower levels, but the gene was not affected in white women living in those same neighborhoods."We're looking at the contribution of genetics to the expression of this tumor suppressor, [and] we know the environment is contributing in some way," Jenkins-Lord says.

In the Atlanta metropolitan area, Jasmine Miller-Kleinhenz, a University of Mississippi Medical Center cancer biologist, found that women with breast cancer living in areas experiencing contemporary redlining, or the systematic denial of mortgage loans based on a location's racial demographics, experienced accelerated biological aging. "That's important because cancer is primarily a disease of aging cells," Miller-Kleinhenz says. Almost 90 percent of Black women in the study lived in redlined areas compared with about 30 percent of white women.

The latest research on breast cancer disparities connects data on socioeconomic characteristics, genetic ancestry and gene expression with health outcomes, Jenkins-Lord says. "It's a gene-versus-environment question, and I think that's where this research is going to continue to go," she says. "Your genetics ... are going to have an impact, but where you live and your exposures over your lifetime are also going to impact the expression of these cancer-related genes."

About the Author

Leah Small is a Richmond, Va.–based freelance journalist whose work has appeared in the Guardian, the New York Times, Virginia Public Media and other outlets.

Scientists Discover Brain Network That May Cause Parkinson's Disease

By Allison Parshall

Scientists have found a key brain network that's disrupted by Parkinson's disease, according to a study published today in *Nature*. The results change doctors' understanding of what causes Parkinson's symptoms and may unlock more effective and precise treatments.

Parkinson's has long been considered a movement disorder. Its hallmark symptoms include involuntary muscle contractions, tremor and difficulty walking. But the disease can also disrupt sleep, blood pressure regulation, digestion and cognitive function. The movement-related symptoms can worsen when someone with the disease is under stress, for example, but improve while they are listening to music.

The common factor underlying these seemingly disconnected symptoms, according to the new results, is a brain network that was only discovered in 2023. Called the somato-cognitive action network, or SCAN, it links the mind and the body to turn thoughts into actions. The researchers found that targeting this network with brain-stimulating treatments could better alleviate the symptoms of Parkinson's disease.

"Parkinson's is not just a movement problem involving one body part. This study shows it is a whole-body brain network disorder that links movement, thinking, arousal and internal body control," says Michael Okun, a neurologist at the University of Florida and medical director of the Parkinson's Foundation, who was not involved in the study.

It's an "extraordinary" set of findings, says Todd Herrington, a neurologist at Massachusetts General Hospital who treats and studies Parkinson's.

A Strange Pattern

Neuroscientists have long known that a region of the brain called the primary motor cortex, nicknamed M1, controls the body's movements. This headband-shaped brain strip extends from ear to ear and contains a "map" of the entire body—often visualized as a distorted humanoid figure called the homunculus. If you want to move your hand, higher-level brain regions closer to your forehead send signals back to M1, which in turn sends motor signals to the hand.

But neurologist Nico Dosenbach of Washington University in St. Louis had observed something strange. When a person in a brain scanner moves their mouth, multiple parts of M1—not just the "mouth" region—activate. These extra spots of activation "just didn't make sense, if all the things I thought I knew were true," he says.

It turns out that neuroscientists had been underestimating M1 for nearly a century. M1 is not a simple map of the body. Interspersed between body-part-specific areas are nodes of a network that coordinates higher-level planning for movement. Instead of being a mere foot soldier following orders from more frontal brain regions, M1 helps plan, guide and coordinate action. Dosenbach and his colleagues named the network the somato-cognitive action network, or SCAN, reflecting how it bridges the body and the mind.

These findings caught the eye of Hesheng Liu, a neuroscientist at Changping Laboratory in Beijing. For a decade, he'd been studying Parkinson's disease, trying to figure out how a treatment called deep-brain stimulation (DBS) works to alleviate symptoms. His team had noticed the strange patterns in M1, too. "We had no idea what they are," Liu says. When he saw Dosenbach's paper on SCAN, everything started to make sense. "Probably, that region is behind Parkinson's disease," he thought.

A Mind-Body Network

Doctors don't know what sets off the chain of events that cause Parkinson's disease. But they know which brain area it most devastates: the substantia nigra, a structure deep in the brain, where neurons that produce the brain signaling chemical dopamine slowly die off.

Stimulating other regions connected to the substantia nigra can alleviate Parkinson's symptoms, suggesting an entire circuit is involved. Researchers knew that M1 was part of this circuit–and the new results show that it specifically involves the SCAN regions of M1 that plan and coordinate movement. Using multiple brain-imaging datasets from 863 real people with Parkinson's and healthy individuals, Liu's team found that SCAN was overlyconnected to deep-brain regions in those with Parkinson's but not in healthy people or those with other movement disorders. Individuals with Parkinson's who had higher connectivity in this circuit experienced worse symptoms.

The researchers also found that existing treatments for Parkinson's, including the medication levodopa (also known as L-DOPA), as well as brain stimulation, decreased the circuit's connectivity, making the brains of people with the condition look more like those of healthy people. The more a treatment reduced someone's SCAN connectivity, the more their motor function improved.

Doctors don't yet know if dying neurons in the substantia nigra cause these SCAN disruptions, or vice versa, says Michael D. Fox, a neurologist at Brigham and Women's Hospital in Boston, who was not involved in the study. Neurons begin dying decades before symptoms appear, so it seems likely that the former may cause the latter. But it's "not impossible" that the SCAN dysfunction could start early, too, and cause more neurons to die, he says.

Guiding Better Treatment

Brain stimulation treatments for Parkinson's were more effective when doctors specifically targeted SCAN regions, Liu's team also found. This experiment involved a noninvasive technique called transcranial magnetic stimulation, or TMS, in which doctors place a wand containing a magnetic coil over the scalp, just on top of M1. Previous studies had shown that the treatment improved symptoms but wasn't more effective than the medication levodopa. In part because of that limitation, Fox says, TMS isn't offered clinically to people with Parkinson's.

But focusing TMS on SCAN regions specifically can improve results, Liu's team showed. "I'm excited by these results," Fox says. TMS may be more appealing and accessible to patients than deep-brain stimulation, which requires surgery. "This, in my mind, elevates the potential of noninvasive brain stimulation for helping patients with Parkinson's in a way that wasn't there before," Fox says.

About the Author

Allison Parshall is associate editor for mind and brain at Scientific American *and she writes the weekly online Science Quizzes. As a multimedia journalist, she contributes to* Scientific American's *podcast* Science Quickly. *Parshall's work has also appeared in* Quanta Magazine *and Inverse. She graduated from New York University's Arthur L. Carter Journalism Institute with a master's degree in science, health and environmental reporting. She has a bachelor's degree in psychology from Georgetown University.*

Scientists Create the Smallest-Ever Moving Cell

By Saugat Bolakhe

As a child, Makoto Miyata loved tinkering with radios and amplifiers. Now his interest in fiddling with things has only grown—but as a cellular biologist, he does it at a much finer scale. For a paper in *Science Advances*, Miyata's team at Osaka Metropolitan University in Japan has tweaked the genes of the smallest synthetic life-form to make it move on its own, hinting at how minimal genetic additions could have helped primordial cells begin to move.

Researchers have long been working to understand how the earliest natural cells might have developed movement. Such studies have used the bacterial genus *Spiroplasma*: single-celled, helix-shaped parasitic microbes that move by simply bending, flexing and changing their shape—not by using specialized appendages, as many other bacteria do. In *Spiroplasma*, scientists had already identified seven genes likely to aid this kind of cell movement. But confirming these genes' precise roles experimentally has proved challenging.

The team turned to a synthetic cell, called JCVI-syn3.0 (syn3.0 for short), which researchers at the J. Craig Venter Institute created in 2016. The cell survives and replicates with a record-breakingly small total of 473 genes—humans, by comparison, have more than 20,000. But syn3.0 can't move.

Miyata and his colleagues inserted combinations of the seven movement-associated *Spiroplasma* genes into syn3.0 cells. He says he vividly remembers the moment he peered through a microscope and saw the previously stationary synthetic cells "dancing." Nearly half had taken on new shapes; some had even developed twisting helical forms to swim, just like *Spiroplasma*.

Miyata had imagined creating a synthetic cell that could move, but he says it was still "quite surprising" when it actually happened. He wasn't the only one surprised, according to National

Institute of Standards and Technology cellular engineer Elizabeth A. Strychalski, who was not involved in the study but attended a presentation ahead of its release. "When they showed the video of these organisms swimming and how their [shapes] had changed, you could almost feel the collective gasp," she says. Miyata's team found that introducing combinations of just two genes was enough to produce *Spiroplasma*-like movement.

Strychalski notes that other researchers used a similar DNA-insertion technique to add jellyfish fluorescence genes into feline embryos, creating domestic cats that glowed. But few had expected it could work in synthetic cells. This experiment "felt very bold," she says, "and [its success] is also tremendously motivating and uplifting for the field."

Although it's hard to imagine what conditions triggered cells' first movements billions of years ago, this research shows how small changes could help them take that massive leap. The study also has implications for the future, Strychalski says: "Mobile synthetic cells might someday be engineered to seek out contaminants, pathogens or even cancer cells in the human body."

About the Author

Saugat Bolakhe is a freelance science journalist. He studied zoology as an undergraduate in Nepal and received a master's degree from the Craig Newmark Graduate School of Journalism at the City University of New York. His work has appeared in Scientific American, Nature, New Scientist, Quanta, Eos, Discover, Knowable *and other publications.*

2021 Medicine Nobel Prize Winner Explains the Importance of Sensing Touch

By Tanya Lewis

How does your body know where your limbs are when you are not looking at them? How does it sense when it is time to go to the bathroom or whether a touch is soothing or painful?

All these abilities rely on a mechanism for sensing touch or pressure. And this week Ardem Patapoutian of Scripps Research in La Jolla, Calif., was awarded a Nobel Prize in Physiology or Medicine for contributing to the discovery of such mechanisms, which detect these sensory inputs and convert them into neural impulses the brain can perceive. He shared the prize with David Julius of the University of California, San Francisco, whose work revealed how we sense heat and pain.

Patapoutian and his colleagues identified pressure-sensitive ion channels known as Piezo1 and Piezo2—specialized protein molecules embedded in the membranes of some cells that enable them to transmit signals in response to touch or pressure. To find them, the researchers methodically deactivated individual genes in pressure-sensitive cells until they found ones that instruct the cells to make these ion channels, turning off the cells' ability to respond to touch. Then they inserted those genes into cells that were not sensitive to touch and showed that the cells had gained this sensitivity.

This mechanism is critical for everything from knowing the position of one's limbs in space—a sense called proprioception—to detecting bladder fullness and the amount of air in the lungs. Understanding it is a breakthrough for basic science and could one day lead to treatments for disorders of touch or internal organ sensing.

Scientific American spoke with Patapoutian about how he learned he had won a Nobel Prize, why the sense of touch has remained a mystery for so long and why these discoveries are so important for human physiology.

[*An edited transcript of the interview follows.*]

How did you find out you had won a Nobel?

My phone was on "do not disturb" mode, so I almost didn't get the news. My dad is 94 years old, and he lives alone with my mom in Los Angeles. They have a landline, so they got the call. And he was able to call me, so I heard it from my dad–which was a really special moment, actually. I mean, they didn't tell him. He just said, "I think you got it," because of the fact that they called him. But it was a wonderful moment. Even if you think it's a possibility, it's still a complete shock to hear. And it's also two in the morning, so you're worried that you're not coherent at all.

It's been a crazy 24 hours, but I've enjoyed it. This is not just about me but about people in my lab, my institute, the whole field that studies touch. Everybody's having a great time with it.

Why are the senses of temperature and touch so important?

I always like to emphasize that my colleagues and I study we do because of just the interest in basic science. I think it's fascinating how, when we started this, one of the major five senses mechanistically–how we sense touch–was not understood. It's something so unique because everything else–whether you're talking about smell or taste, which are based on chemicals, or hormones being secreted from your body, such as insulin–is chemical sensing. So here is a phenomenon that's completely different, and it's based on sensing physical stimuli such as pressure.

But I also find super fascinating this idea of proprioception: the sense of where your limbs are, compared with the rest of your body. I consider it perhaps your most important sense. I would say the majority of people have probably never even heard of it or have never stopped to think about this sense. Your sensory neurons innervate all the muscles in your body, and from how much your muscles are stretched, you have a very visual–without actually looking–image of where your limbs are. This is how I can close my eyes and touch my nose. This is proprioception. I think, partly, people take it for granted because you can never turn it off. It's not like your vision, where you can close your eyes and say, "This is what the world is like without seeing."

The fact that the senses of temperature, touch and pain are all related and that they're done by the same neuronal [machinery] makes a very compelling case for why it was interesting to study.

Can you give an overview of the research that led to your prize?

The idea was very simple. We knew that for touch to be initiated, there are these pressure-activated ion channels that do something very basic: they're either closed or they're open. And when they open, ions (for example, sodium) come in. That's a language that neurons understand because [the flood of sodium ions] depolarizes a neuron and sends a signal called an action potential, which can then talk to the next neuron. But the identities of these pressure sensors [or receptors] were just not known. That has been the focus of my life for the past 10 years. When we first found the Piezo receptors in 2010, it was because we took a very reductionist approach. We said, "We know there are these pressure sensors in our bodies, but we don't know what they are." And we said, "The easiest way to find them is to find a cell line–a cell that grows in a culture dish–that responds to pressure."

So my [then] postdoctoral scholar Bertrand Coste found a cell line that responds to pressure this way. And he made a list of candidate genes and, one by one, knocked them down [deactivated them] and tried to see if this pressure-sensing response was still there. It was very laborious. It took him about three days to test each candidate, so he had a whole year of negative data. And then, finally, candidate number 73–when he deleted or knocked it down, this pressure response was gone. And so we knew we had something interesting on our hands.

What did you do next to prove that these genes were actually necessary for sensing pressure?

The big experiment was now to take those genes and make a full-length protein and put it in a cell that was not mechanosensitive [touch sensitive]–and every cell we put it in became mechanosensitive. So that's what we call "necessary and sufficient." The two experiments together made a very convincing case that this was the sensor.

What are some of the practical applications of this work?

Within a few years, we showed that these ion channels are the principal sensors for touch sensation, for proprioception, for a specific type of pain sensation that is common in chronic pain conditions. We've also shown that they play a big role in interoception, which is sensing of internal organs. Take bladder fullness: every time you feel like you have to go, it's a mechanical sense–the bladder stretches, and it tells you when you have to go. This seems to be Piezo2-dependent. Every time you breathe, Piezo channels are monitoring how much your lungs are inflating. The list goes on and on. We've also shown that these ion channels sense blood pressure in your blood vessels and are part of a feedback loop to keep your blood pressure constant.

We also collaborate with Alexander Chesler and his colleagues at the National Institutes of Health, who have access to studied individuals who lack Piezo2. Their major phenotype is that they are uncoordinated–they don't learn to walk until they're five years old or older, and even then, they need help doing it. Chesler and his team quickly realized, when they did tests, that these individuals cannot discriminate touch, and their proprioception is completely nonfunctional. They have the same kind of deficits as people with some forms of allodynia, which is when touch becomes painful (for example, if you get a sunburn, just wearing your shirt or touching your shoulder hurts). People who suffer from neuropathic pain experience this phenomenon chronically, and there are really no good medications for it. We've done some tests to show that these conditions are Piezo2-dependent. This is why we think it actually might be an interesting drug target in the future.

There are challenges; these are not easy molecules to target. But more importantly, deactivating Piezo2 all over your body with a pill taken orally is not a good idea. That's going to knock down your sense of touch, proprioception and everything else. So any modulation of this has to be done locally, maybe just within the bladder. Or if you have a very severe neuropathic pain in your elbow or some other body part, I can imagine a topical drug. We're not anywhere close to that yet, but it could be useful.

You grew up in Lebanon during a period of war and violence. How has that influenced your life and career?

I'm of Armenian origin. I grew up in Lebanon, and I pretty much fled to the U.S. when I was 18. I think it has had a huge influence on me. You know, growing up in a war-torn country, I couldn't even imagine having a career in science. Coming here was a great shock, but at the same time, I think it's always been in me not to take things for granted because of my tough childhood and all the things that I experienced. I think that's helped me in appreciating what I have and knowing what a privilege it is to get the education I've gotten here–to have the government fund basic science, which I think is a no-brainer in the sense that not only are discoveries great, but all practical applications come from basic discoveries. And I think the U.S. is still one of the best places in the world that encourages this.

About the Author

Tanya Lewis is senior desk editor for health and medicine at Scientific American. *She writes and edits stories for the website and print magazine on topics ranging from COVID to organ transplants. She also appears on* Scientific American's *podcast* Science Quickly *and writes* Scientific American's *weekly Health & Medicine newsletter. She has held a number of positions over her nine years at* Scientific American, *including health editor, assistant news editor and associate editor at* Scientific American Mind. *Previously, she has written for outlets that include* Insider, Wired, Science News *and others. She has a degree in biomedical engineering from Brown University and one in science communication from the University of California, Santa Cruz. Follow her on Bluesky @tanyalewis.bsky.social*

China's Giant Underground Neutrino Observatory Just Released Its First Results—And They're Promising

By Jeanna Bryner

Trillions of neutrinos whiz through our bodies every day, pulsing from the sun, outer space and deep beneath Earth. Yet these elusive subatomic particles have proven difficult to study. That could soon change, however. Buried 700 meters beneath the rolling hills of southern China, an enormous neutrino observatory called JUNO has released its first results after a mere 59 days of operation. And so far, they are very promising, physicists say.

"The physics result is already world-leading in the areas that it touches," says particle physicist Juan Pedro Ochoa-Ricoux of the University of California, Irvine, who co-leads a team on JUNO.

"In particular, we measured two neutrino oscillation parameters, and that measurement is already for both parameters the best in the world," he says. The results were published in two separate preprints on arXiv.org.

JUNO—short for Jiangmen Underground Neutrino Observatory—has been tasked with a tall order: determine the ordering of masses of the three types of neutrino. In other words, do they follow a "normal mass ordering," where the first flavor of neutrino is the lightest and the third the heaviest, or an inverted one, in which the third neutrino mass state is the lightest?

The answer to this question holds myriad implications, from informing other experiments to uncovering new physics to explaining certain cosmological mysteries. That's because despite being such lightweights, neutrinos are so incredibly numerous that they may play an outsized role in the distribution of matter in the universe.

JUNO's spherical detector, which is akin to a 13-story-tall fishbowl, primarily measures so-called electron antineutrinos spewing from the nearby Yangjian and Taishan nuclear plants. When the particles strike a proton inside the detector, a reaction triggers two light flashes that ping photomultiplier tubes and get converted into electrical signals.

The new measurements from these neutrino-proton collisions are now considered the most precise for two oscillation parameters, which act as proxies for differences in their mass, according to Ochoa-Ricoux.

"It is the first time we've turned on a scientific instrument like JUNO that we've been working on for over a decade. It's just tremendously exciting," Ochoa-Ricoux says. "And then to see that we're able to already do world-leading measurements with it, even with such a small amount of data, that's also really exciting."

Still, the physicists will need years' worth of neutrino detections to answer the mass-ordering conundrum.

About the Author

Jeanna Bryner is executive editor of Scientific American. *Previously she was editor in chief of Live Science and, prior to that, an editor at Scholastic's* Science World *magazine. Bryner has an English degree from Salisbury University, a master's degree in biogeochemistry and environmental sciences from the University of Maryland and a graduate science journalism degree from New York University. She has worked as a biologist in Florida, where she monitored wetlands and did field surveys for endangered species, including the gorgeous Florida Scrub Jay. She also received an ocean sciences journalism fellowship from the Woods Hole Oceanographic Institution. She is a firm believer that science is for everyone and that just about everything can be viewed through the lens of science.*

Is It Time to Redefine Time?

By Jay Bennett

Inside a laboratory nestled in the foothills of the Rocky Mountains, amid a labyrinth of lenses, mirrors, and other optical machinery bolted to a vibration-resistant table, an apparatus resembling a chimney pipe rises toward the ceiling. On a recent visit, the silvery pipe held a cloud of thousands of supercooled cesium atoms launched upward by lasers and then left to float back down. With each cycle, a maser–like a laser that produces microwaves–hit the atoms to send their outer electrons jumping to a different energy state.

The machine, called a cesium fountain clock, was in the middle of a two-week measurement run at a National Institute of Standards and Technology (NIST) research facility in Boulder, Colo., repeatedly fountaining atoms. Detectors inside measured photons released by the atoms as they settled back down to their original states. Atoms make such transitions by absorbing a specific amount of energy and then emitting it in the form of a specific frequency of light, meaning the light's waves always reach their peak amplitude at a regular, dependable cadence. This cadence provides a natural temporal reference that scientists can pinpoint with extraordinary precision.

By repeating the fountain process hundreds of thousands of times, the instrument narrows in on the exact transition frequency of the cesium atoms. Although it's technically a clock, the cesium fountain could not tell you the hour. "This instrument does not keep track of time," says Vladislav Gerginov, a senior research associate at NIST and the keeper of this clock. "It's a frequency reference–a tuning fork." By tuning a beam of light to match this resonance frequency, metrologists can "realize time," as they phrase it, counting the oscillations of the light wave.

The signal from this tuning fork–about nine gigahertz–is used to calibrate about 18 smaller atomic clocks at NIST that run 24 hours a day. Housed in egg incubators to control the temperature and humidity, these clocks maintain the official time for the U.S., which is compared with similar measurements in other countries to set Coordinated Universal Time, or UTC.

Gerginov, dressed casually in a short-sleeve plaid shirt and sneakers, spoke of the instrument with an air of pride. He had recently replaced the clock's microwave cavity, a copper passageway in the middle of the pipe where the atoms interact with the maser. The instrument would soon be christened NIST-F4, the new principal reference clock for the U.S. "It's going to be the primary standard of frequency," Gerginov says, looking up at the metallic fountain, a three-foot-tall vacuum chamber with four layers of nickel-iron-alloy magnetic shielding. "Until the definition of the second changes."

Since 1967 the second has been defined as the duration of 9,192,631,770 cycles of cesium's resonance frequency. In other words, when the outer electron of a cesium atom falls to the lower state and releases light, the amount of time it takes to emit 9,192,631,770 cycles of the light wave defines one second. "You can think of an atom as a pendulum," says NIST research fellow John Kitching. "We cause the atoms to oscillate at their natural resonance frequency. Every atom of cesium is the same, and the frequencies don't change. They're determined by fundamental constants. And that's why atomic clocks are the best way of keeping time right now."

But cesium clocks are no longer the most accurate clocks available. In the past five years the world's most advanced atomic clocks have reached a critical milestone by taking measurements that are more than two orders of magnitude more accurate than those of the best cesium clocks. These newer instruments, called optical clocks, use different atoms, such as strontium or ytterbium, that transition at much higher frequencies. They release optical light, as opposed to the microwave light given out by cesium, effectively dividing the second into about 50,000 times as many "ticks" as a cesium clock can measure.

The fact that optical clocks have surpassed the older atomic clocks has created something of a paradox. The new clocks can measure time more accurately than a cesium clock–but cesium clocks define time. The duration of one second is inherently linked to the transition frequency of cesium. Until a redefinition occurs, nothing can truly be a more accurate second because 9,192,631,770 cycles of cesium's resonance frequency is what a second is.

This problem is why many scientists believe it is time for a new definition of the second. In 2024 a task force set up by the International Bureau of Weights and Measures (BIPM), headquartered in Sèvres, France, released a road map that established criteria for redefining the second. These include that the new standard is measured by at least three different clocks at different institutions, that those measurements are routinely compared with values from other types of clocks and that laboratories around the world will be able to build their own clocks to measure the target frequency. If sufficient progress is made on the criteria in the next two years, then the second might change as soon as 2030.

But not everyone is onboard with redefining the second now. For one thing, there's no clear immediate benefit. Today's cesium clocks are plenty accurate enough for most practical applications–including synchronizing the GPS satellites we all depend on. We can always improve the accuracy of the second later if new innovations come along that require better timing. "Today we don't really profit from an immediate change," says Nils Huntemann, a scientist at the Physikalisch-Technische Bundesanstalt (PTB), the national metrology institute of Germany. Redefining the second wouldn't be straightforward, either–scientists would be forced to pick a new standard from the many advanced atomic clocks now in existence, with improvements being made all the time. How should they choose?

Many scientists say we should improve the definition of time simply because we can.

Regardless of the complications, some physicists believe that they have an obligation to use the best clocks available. "It's just a matter of basic principle," says Elizabeth Donley, chief of the time and frequency division at NIST. "You want to allow for the best measurements you can possibly make."

The world's first clocks were invented thousands of years ago, when the first human civilizations devised devices that tracked the sun's movement to divide the day into intervals. The earliest versions of sundials were made by the ancient Egyptians around 1500 B.C.E. Later, water clocks, first used by Egyptians and called *clepsydras*, meaning "water thieves," by the ancient Greeks, marked time by letting water drain out of vessels with a hole punched in the bottom. These instruments were perhaps the first to measure a duration of time independent of the movements of celestial bodies. Mechanical clocks driven by weights debuted in medieval European churches, and they ticked along at consistent rates, leading to the modern 24-hour day. The tolling of bells to mark the hour even gave us the word "clock," which has its roots in the Latin *clocca*, meaning "bell."

As mechanical clocks became more precise, particularly with the development of the pendulum clock in the mid-17th century, timekeepers further divided the hour into minutes and seconds. (First applied to angular degrees, the word "minute" comes from the Latin *prima minuta*, meaning the "first small part," and "second" comes from *secunda minuta*, the "second small part.") For centuries towns maintained their own local clocks, adjusting them periodically so the strike of noon occurred just as the sundial indicated midday. It wasn't until the 19th century, when distant rail stations needed to maintain coordinated train schedules, that time zones were established and timekeeping was standardized around the world.

Clocks improved drastically in the 20th century after French physicists and brothers Jacques and Pierre Curie discovered that applying an electric current to a crystal of quartz causes it to vibrate with a stable frequency. The first clock that used a quartz oscillator was developed by Warren Marrison and Joseph Horton of Bell Laboratories in 1927. The clock ran a current through quartz and used a circuit to divide the resulting frequency until it was low enough to drive a synchronous motor that controlled the clock's face. Today billions of quartz clocks are produced every year for wristwatches, mobile devices, computers, and other electronics.

The key innovation that led to atomic clocks came from American physicist Isidor Isaac Rabi of Columbia University, who won the Nobel Prize in Physics in 1944 for developing a way to precisely measure atoms' resonance frequencies. His technique, called the molecular-beam magnetic resonance method, finely tuned a radio frequency to cause atoms' quantum states to transition. In 1939 Rabi suggested using this method to build a clock, and the next year his colleagues at Columbia applied his technique to determine the resonance frequency of cesium.

This element was viewed as an ideal reference atom for timekeeping. It's a soft, silvery metal that is liquid near room temperature, similar to mercury. Cesium is a relatively heavy element, meaning it moves more slowly than lighter elements and is therefore easier to observe. Its resonance frequency is also higher than those of other clock candidates of the time, such as rubidium and hydrogen, meaning it had the potential to create a more precise time standard. These properties eventually won cesium the role of defining the second nearly 40 years later.

But the first atomic clock was not a cesium clock. In 1949 Harold Lyons, a physicist at's precursor, the National Bureau of Standards (NBS), built an atomic clock based on Rabi's magnetic resonance method using ammonia molecules. It looked like a computer rack with a series of gauges and dials on it, so Lyons affixed a clockface to the top for a public demonstration to indicate that his machine was, in fact, a clock. This first atomic clock, however, couldn't match the precision of the best quartz clocks of the time, and ammonia was abandoned when it became clear that cesium clocks would produce better results.

Both the NBS and the National Physical Laboratory (NPL) in the U.K. developed cesium beam clocks in the 1950s. A key breakthrough came from Harvard University physicist Norman Ramsey, who found that it was possible to improve the measurements by using two pulses of microwaves to induce the atomic transitions rather than one. Cesium clocks continued to advance for the remainder of the century and, along with atomic clocks using different elements, became more precise and more compact.

At the time, the second was defined according to astronomical time. Known as the ephemeris second, it was equal to 1/31,556,925.9747 of the tropical year (the time it takes for the sun to return to the same position in the sky) in 1900. Between 1955 and 1958, NPL scientists compared measurements from their cesium beam clock with the ephemeris second as measured by the U.S. Naval Observatory by tracking the position of the moon with respect to background stars. In August 1958 the second was calculated as 9,192,631,770 cycles of the cesium transition frequency—the same number that would be used for the new definition nine years later.

Since then, atomic clocks have continued to progress, particularly with the development of cesium fountain clocks in the 1980s. But by 2006 newer clocks were beating them.

In addition to the clocks at NIST, some of the most advanced timekeepers in the world can be found at the University of Colorado Boulder, down the street in another lab pushing the frontier of timekeeping. JILA, a joint venture of NIST and the university, houses four "optical lattice clocks" that are among the global record holders for accuracy. (The lab was previously called the Joint Institute for Laboratory Astrophysics and now is simply known by the acronym.)

These state-of-the-art instruments are housed in large rectangular boxes with sliding doors that double as dry-erase boards, each covered in equations and diagrams. Components twinkle in the dim light of the lab as lasers and readout devices pulse with light.

Each clock works by firing two lasers at each other to create an interference pattern called an optical lattice, a grid with areas of high and low intensity. Pancake-shaped clouds of thousands of neutral strontium atoms become trapped in the high-intensity parts of the lattice, suspended in place.

Another laser then induces an electron transition in the atoms, pushing the outer electrons up an entire orbital level. This is a larger transition than occurs in the cesium atoms, where the electrons only move up one "hyperfine" level. But as in the cesium clock, detectors look for photons released when the electrons settle back to their original states to confirm that the laser is at the correct frequency to make the electrons hop. Compared with the cesium transition, which occurs at about nine billion hertz, the strontium transition requires a much higher frequency: 429,228,004,229,873.65 Hz.

Each of the four clocks in the lab serves a different purpose, measuring interactions between the atoms or effects from the environment–such as gravity, temperature fluctuations or wayward electromagnetic fields–in an attempt to reduce these sources of uncertainty. Optical clocks are so sensitive that the slightest disturbance, even someone slamming a nearby door, will shift the target transition frequency.

The key limiting factor in an optical lattice clock is blackbody radiation, says Jun Ye, lead researcher of the JILA lab. This radiation is the thermal energy released by any body of mass because of its temperature alone. To compensate for this effect, Ye and his team built a new thermal-control system inside the vacuum chamber of one of the clocks, a "fairly heroic effort" that Ye attributes to his students. The project allowed them to measure the transition frequency of strontium with a systematic uncertainty of 8.1×10^{-19}, the most accurate clock measurement ever made. This strontium optical lattice clock and other, similar models are now among the leading candidates to redefine the second.

The other main contenders are called single-ion clocks. Some of the best examples can be found at NIST and at the German PTB lab. This type suspends one charged ion (in this case, an atom with one or more electrons removed so that it carries a positive charge) within a trap of electromagnetic fields and then induces an atomic transition with a laser. Currently the most accurate of these clocks uses an aluminum ion.

Single-ion clocks avoid the noise that light lattices introduce to a system, Huntemann says, and "there is generally a smaller sensitivity to external fields," including fields in the experiment as well as the environment. Optical lattice clocks, however, scrutinize thousands of atoms at once, improving accuracy.

Huntemann is researching ways to trap and measure multiple ions at once, such as strontium and ytterbium ions, within the same clock. This approach would allow scientists to probe two different atomic transitions simultaneously, and the clock could average its frequency measurements more quickly–though not as fast as an optical lattice clock.

Ion clocks and optical lattice clocks have been trading the accuracy record back and forth for the past two decades. They have even demonstrated how time passes faster at higher elevations–a prediction from Einstein's general theory of relativity, which showed that time dilates, or stretches, closer to large masses (in this case, Earth). In a 2022 experiment, parts of a strontium optical lattice clock at JILA separated by just a millimeter in height measured a time difference on the order of 0.0000000000000000001 (10^{-19}). This tiny aberration would have been too small for a cesium clock to detect.

If scientists choose to redefine the second, they must decide not only which clock to use but also which atomic transition: that of strontium atoms or ytterbium or aluminum ions–or something else. One possible solution is to base the definition on not just one atomic transition but the average of all the transitions from different kinds of optical clocks. If an ensemble of clocks, each with its own statistical weighting, is used to redefine the second, then future clocks could be added to the definition as needed.

Last year Ye and his team demonstrated the viability of a nuclear clock based on thorium. This type of clock uses a nuclear transition–a shift in the quantum state of atomic nuclei–rather than an electron transition. Because nuclei are less sensitive to external interference than electrons are, nuclear clocks may become even more accurate than optical clocks once the technology is refined.

If the second doesn't get redefined in 2030, scientists can try again in 2034 and 2038 at the next two meetings of the General Conference on Weights and Measures. A new definition won't change much, if anything, for most people, but it will eventually and inevitably lead to technological advances. Researchers are already dreaming up applications such as quantum communication networks or upgraded GPS satellites that could pinpoint any location on Earth to within a centimeter. Other uses are just starting to be envisioned.

By pushing clocks forward, scientists may do more than redefine time–they might redefine our understanding of the universe. Supersensitive clocks that can detect minute changes in the passing of time–as shown in the time-dilation experiment–could be used to detect gravitational waves that pass through Earth as a consequence of massive cataclysms in space. By mapping the gravitational distortion of spacetime more precisely than ever, such clocks could also be used to study dark matter–the missing mass thought to be ubiquitous in the cosmos–as well as how gravity interacts with quantum theory.

Such endeavors could even rewrite our understanding of time itself–which has always been a more complicated notion in physics than in practical life. "The underlying classical laws say that there is no intrinsic difference between the past and future nor any intrinsic direction of determination from past to future," says Jenann Ismael, a philosopher of science at Johns Hopkins University.

In any case, now that we have clocks that outstrip the literal definition of the second, many scientists say the way forward is obvious: we should improve the definition of time simply because we can. "As with any new idea in science, even if it is not exactly clear who needs a better measurement, when a better measurement is available, then you find the application," says Patrizia Tavella, director of the time department at BIPM, the organization that defines the International System of Units. "We can do better," she says of the current second. "Let's do better."

About the Author

Jay Bennett is a science writer based in Copenhagen. He previously worked as a science editor at National Geographic, Smithsonian *and* Popular Mechanics.

Section 3: Advances in Technology

In One Life-Changing Moment, This Former Seaman Jumped from Ships to Computer Chips

By Marlene Stewart

Laeon Israel is a professional cybersleuth. As a senior forensic analyst at Charles Schwab, he is responsible for bringing to light information that will be used in the prosecution of financial crimes. And he came to this by way of an aircraft carrier.

In the 1990s Israel was a Navy deck seaman onboard the U.S.S. *Enterprise*. His role was to help with the upkeep of the physical ship–all 1,123 feet of it. He said it was a moment in one of the ship's computer labs that completely changed his course. "I logged on to the computer and started to see things," he says. "I took a look at the people who were working in the department..., and I said to myself, 'What are you doing?'"

Israel was in paint and grease-smeared coveralls. The people hesaw were in "pressed pants, ironed shirts–they looked sharp," he says. But the difference in garb just snapped his mind to attention. What drew him in were the answers he got to the flood of questions he let loose at his shipmates working at the computer lab. Operating systems, electrical circuits, Internet connectivity, cryptography–immersed in these subjects, he found the start of his path in computer science and his conversion to a career in STEM (science, technology, engineering and mathematics).

When asked about whether his current experience in STEM differs from when he first entered the field, Israel explains that some things have changed for the better–and others have not. He believes that the tech industry is now very "fertile" for people looking for a career.

He also sees the need for more progress. "In STEM, there are still disparities in regards to people of color," he says. "As long as we keep pushing and moving the ball forward, there'll be change, there will be better days." And he points to his employer as a shining example of a corporation that is trying to close the diversity gap in real time.

But one company alone does not constitute the sea change that Israel wants. He still believes that the topic of diversity, equity and inclusion in STEM should be a priority in many industries. To him, that also means that many science- and technology-focused industries still feel unwelcoming to people of color. Yet recent events–such as the murder of George Floyd–have led to what he calls "a renewed spark in education and racial inequality." For Israel, the question remains: When this wave fades, what happens next?

This discussion is part of a speaker series hosted by the Black Employee Network at *Springer Nature*, the publisher of *Scientific American*. The series aims to highlight Black contributions to STEM–a history that has not been widely recognized. It will cover career paths, role models and mentorship, and diversity in STEM.

About the Author

Marlene Stewart is a senior business development manager for Springer Nature based in London, where she is responsible for an international client base. She is U.K. lead of the Springer Nature Black Employee Network and co-leader of the Black table talk program behind this speaker series.

One of the Biggest Problems in Biology Has Finally Been Solved

By Tanya Lewis

There's an age-old adage in biology: structure determines function. To understand the function of the myriad proteins that perform vital jobs in a healthy body—or malfunction in a diseased one—scientists have to first determine these proteins' molecular structure. But this is no easy feat: protein molecules consist of long, twisty chains of up to thousands of amino acids, chemical compounds that can interact with one another in many ways to take on an enormous number of possible three-dimensional shapes. Figuring out a single protein's structure, or solving the "protein-folding problem," can take years of finicky experiments.

But last year an artificial-intelligence program called AlphaFold, developed by the Alphabet-owned company DeepMind, predicted the 3-D structures of almost every known protein—about 200 million in all. DeepMind CEO Demis Hassabis and senior staff research scientist John Jumper were jointly awarded one of this year's $3-million Breakthrough Prizes in Life Sciences for the achievement, which opens the door for applications that range from expanding our understanding of basic molecular biology to accelerating drug development.

DeepMind developed AlphaFold soon after its AlphaGo AI made headlines in 2016 by beating world Go champion Lee Sedol at the game. But the goal was always to develop AI that could tackle important problems in science, Hassabis says. DeepMind has made the structures of proteins from nearly every species for which amino acid sequences exist freely available in a public database.

Scientific American spoke with Hassabis about developing AlphaFold, some of its most exciting potential applications and the ethical considerations of highly sophisticated AI.

[*An edited transcript of the interview follows.*]

Why did you decide to create Alpha-Fold, and how did you get to the point where it can now fold practically every known protein?

We pretty much started the project roughly the day after we came back from the AlphaGo match in Seoul, where we beat Lee Sedol, the world [Go] champion. I was talking to Dave Silver, the project lead on AlphaGo, and we were discussing "What's the next big project that DeepMind should do?" I was feeling like it was time to tackle something really hard in science because we had just solved more or less the pinnacle of games AI. I wanted to finally apply the AI to real-world domains. That's always been the mission of DeepMind: to develop general-purpose algorithms that could be applied across many, many problems. We started off with games because it was more efficient to develop AI and test things out in games for various reasons. But ultimately that was never the end goal. The end goal was to develop things like AlphaFold.

It's been a mammoth project–about five or six years' worth of work before CASP14 [the 14th Critical Assessment of Structure Prediction, a protein-folding competition]. We had an earlier version at the CASP13 competition, and that was AlphaFold 1. That was state of the art, you know, a good deal better than anyone had done before and I think one of the first times that machine learning had been used as the core component of a system to try to crack this problem. That gave us the confidence to push it even further. We had to reengineer things for AlphaFold 2 and put a whole bunch of new ideas in there and also bring onto the team some more specialists–biologists and chemists and biophysicists who worked in protein folding–and combine them with our engineering and machine-learning team.

I've been working on and thinking about general AI for my entire career, even back at university. I tend to note down scientific problems I think one day could be amenable to the types of algorithms we build, and protein folding was right up there for me always, since the 1990s. I've had many, many biologist friends who used to go on about this to me all the time.

Were you surprised that AlphaFold was so successful?

Yeah, it was surprising, actually. It's definitely been the hardest thing we've done, and I would also say the most complex system we've ever built. The *Nature* paper that describes all the methods, with the supplementary information and technical details, is 60 pages long. There are 32 different component algorithms, and each of them is needed. It's a pretty complicated architecture, and it needed a lot of innovation. That's why it took so long. It was important to have all these different inputs from different backgrounds and disciplines. And I think something we do uniquely well at DeepMind is mix that together–not just machine learning and engineering.

But there was a difficult period after AlphaFold 1. We first tried to push AlphaFold 1 to the maximum. And we realized about six months after CASP13 that it was not going to reach the atomic accuracy we wanted to actually solve the problem and be useful to experimentalists and biologists. So I made the decision that we needed to go back to the drawing board and take the knowledge we had acquired, including where it worked and where it didn't work, and then see if we could go back to almost a brainstorming stage with that experience and that knowledge and come up with a whole bunch of new ideas and new architectures. We did that, and ultimately that worked.

But for about six months to a year after that reset, things got worse, not better. The AlphaFold 2 system, the early one, was much worse than AlphaFold 1. It can be very scary during the period where you seem to be going backward in terms of accuracy. Fortunately, that's where our experience in games and all the other AI systems we built before came into play. I'd seen us go through that valley of death and then get out the other side.

Can you explain, on a very simple level, how AlphaFold works?

It's a pretty complicated thing. And we don't know a lot of things for sure. It's clear that AlphaFold 2 is learning something implicit about the structure of chemistry and physics. It sort of knows what things might be plausible. It's learned that through seeing real protein structures, the ones that we know of. But one of the innovations we had was to do something called self-distillation, which is to get an early version of AlphaFold 2 to predict lots of structures—and to predict the confidence level in those predictions.

One of the things we built in was this understanding of chemical bond angles, as well as evolutionary history, using a process called multisequence alignment. These bring in some constraints, which help to narrow the search space of possible protein structures. The search space is too huge to solve it by brute force. But obviously real-world physics solves this somehow because proteins fold up in nanoseconds or milliseconds. Effectively, we're trying to reverse engineer that process by learning from the output examples. I think AlphaFold has captured something quite deep about the physics and the chemistry of molecules.

The fascinating thing about AI in general is that it's kind of a black box. But ultimately it seems like it's learning actual rules about the natural world.

Yeah, it's almost learning about it in an intuitive sense. I think we'll have more and more researchers looking at protein areas that AlphaFold is not good at predicting and asking, "Are they actually disordered in biology when the protein doesn't have a clear shape, when it's not interacting with something?" About 30 percent of proteins [from organisms with a nucleus] are thought to be disordered. A lot of those kinds of proteins are implicated in disease, such as neurodegeneration, because they might get tangled. And you can see how they might do so because they're just sort of floppy strings rather than forming structures.

The other extremely important thing we did with AlphaFold 2, which we don't do with machine-learning systems, was output a confidence measure on every single amino acid because we wanted a biologist to be able to know which parts of the prediction they could rely on without needing to understand anything about the machine learning.

What are some of AlphaFold's most exciting applications?

We have a lot of nice case studies from partners—early adopters—that have had a year to work with AlphaFold. They're doing an incredibly diverse set of things, from addressing antibiotic resistance to tackling plastic pollution by designing plastic-eating enzymes. I've been talking to [CRISPR gene-editing pioneer] Jennifer Doudna about alfalfa crop sustainability—her team is trying to engineer crops to be a bit more sustainable in the face of climate change.

There's also lots of very cool fundamental research being done with it. There was an entire special issue of *Science* on how scientists solved the structure of the nuclear pore complex. This group of membrane-spanning proteins in the nucleus of eukaryotic cells is one of the biggest proteins in the body. Several groups solved it at the same time from the cryo-EM [cryogenic electron microscopy] data—but they all needed AlphaFold predictions to augment those data in some places. So a combination of experimental structural data with AlphaFold turns out to be a boon to structural biologists, which we weren't necessarily predicting.

And then in practical terms, almost every pharma company we've talked to is using AlphaFold. We'll probably never know what the full impacts are because obviously they keep that proprietary. But I like to think we've helped accelerate drug development and cures for diseases by a few years.

There's been a lot of hype around AI and everything it can do, especially for science and medicine. But AlphaFold seems to have a clear benefit.

I mean, it's for you to decide. But I would say I've had a lot of people tell me that it's the most concrete, useful case of AI doing something in science. I like the fact that we're delivering on the promise of AI. I mean, you could say "hype," but we try and let our work speak for itself.

I remember when we started in 2010, nobody was working on AI. And 12 years later it seems like everyone and their dog are talking about it. And in most cases, as I'm sure you have to sift through all the time, it's like they don't know what AI even is sometimes, or they're misusing the term, or it's not that impressive what's going on. But I think AlphaFold is a very good proof of concept or role model of what could happen. And I think we're going to see much more of that in the next decade–of AI helping to genuinely accelerate some scientific breakthroughs–and we hope to be part of a lot more. We think it's just the beginning.

AI has been in the news a lot lately, whether for producing intelligent language or creating digital art. As AI becomes a bigger part of our lives, how should we think about its consequences?

We at DeepMind have our own internal versions of large language models and text-to-image systems, and we'll probably be releasing some of them at some point [in 2023]. It's really interesting seeing the explosion of developments. AlphaFold, obviously, is huge in the scientific community. But with language and image AIs, it's starting to break through into the mainstream. Everyone, of course, knows about language and can appreciate images–you don't have to have any scientific expertise.

But I think we should always be thinking about the ethical issues, and that's one reason we haven't released our language-based AI yet. We're trying to be responsible about really checking what these models can do–how they can go off the rails, what happens if they're toxic, all of these things that are currently top of mind. It's our view that some of these systems are not ready to release to the general public, at least not unrestricted. But at some point, that's going to happen. We have this phrase at DeepMind of "pioneering responsibly." And for me, that's about applying the scientific method to analyzing and building these systems. I think often, especially in Silicon Valley, there's this sort of hacker mentality that "we'll just hack it and put it out there and then see what happens." I think that's exactly the wrong approach for technologies as impactful and potentially powerful as AI.

I've worked on AI my entire life because I think it's going to be the most beneficial thing ever for humanity, for things like curing diseases, helping with climate change, all of this stuff. But it's a dual-use technology: it depends on how, as a society, we decide to deploy it–and what we use it for.

And I think we're seeing the consequences of that with social media.

How is AI being used–or misused– in social media?

It's not proper AI; it's more statistical algorithms. But we've seen the unintended consequences for democracies. Probably the people who created the social media platforms did not have bad intent when they started; it just kind of got out of hand. But we want to make sure that we think about those knock-on effects early, before going, "Oh, oops, this happened," and then trying to bolt the barn door after the horses have left. We shouldn't do that with powerful technologies. We can take some inspiration and advice from, for example, CRISPR and other technologies. I think there are things we can learn from other scientific communities that have tackled these questions.

About the Author

Tanya Lewis is senior desk editor for health and medicine at Scientific American. *She writes and edits stories for the website and print magazine on topics ranging from COVID to organ transplants. She also appears on* Scientific American's *podcast* Science Quickly *and writes* Scientific American's *weekly Health & Medicine newsletter. She has held a number of positions over her nine years at* Scientific American, *including health editor, assistant news editor and associate editor at* Scientific American Mind. *Previously, she has written for outlets that include* Insider, Wired, Science News *and others. She has a degree in biomedical engineering from Brown University and one in science communication from the University of California, Santa Cruz. Follow her on Bluesky @tanyalewis.bsky.social*

Scientists Turned 300,000 Litter Box Visits into an AI-Powered Cat Health Monitor

By Deni Ellis Béchard

To cat owners, a litter box is a nuisance. But to scientists, it's a trove of information. A team of researchers at Nestlé Purina PetCare decided to investigate litter boxes as records of behavior: the pre-squat scratch, the whirl, the precise geometry of the bury.

The scientists built a painstaking dictionary of these gestures—a full "ethogram," or catalog, of species-specific behaviors—and then identified the distinct moves in feline bathroom habits: grooming, digging, sniffing litter. "We landed on 39 different behaviors that cats do in a litter box, with the understanding that depending on their satisfaction with the litter box, the environment and the dynamics around them, those behaviors will shift," says Ragen McGowan, director of digital and AI product development at Purina and one of the authors of a paper published recently in *Applied Animal Behaviour Science* on the development of Purina's AI-powered litter box monitor. "We realized this ethogram could be a window into their health."

Cats commonly suffer from diabetes, obesity, kidney disease, hyperthyroidism, urinary tract infections and many more conditions. The researchers hoped to predict and stave off these ailments by training an artificial intelligence system on everything a cat can do in a litter box. They believed that AI could warn cat owners of feline health concerns long before the cats—ever stoic and aloof—showed signs.

But arriving at the 39 behavior types wasn't easy. The project began in 2018. The team gathered data from 191 cats—140 at a company research center in Missouri and 51 in private homes. The researchers placed scales with a sensor at each corner that could detect tiny changes in weight and movement under litter boxes. They then made video recordings of every bathroom visit so that artificial intelligence could correlate the visual data with the weight and movements that the sensors recorded. But for the AI to do that, the scientists first had to generate the ethogram.

Watching the videos, they labeled every nudge and movement, peering at ear angles, at the bunching or flaring of whiskers. If you've ever watched a cat rotate exactly three and a half times before committing to a square inch of litter, you begin to understand the research process–multiplied hundreds of thousands of times. "We took over 300,000 videos of cats eliminating in different scenarios–single cat, multicat, all different types of litter boxes," McGowan says.

The team then paired those video labels with the weight and movement data so that the AI could distinguish a quick tinkle from a philosophical contemplation. "We would work closely with our behaviorists to discuss what they're looking at in the videos, and then we had to develop mathematical equations," says Natalie Langenfeld-McCoy, manager of AI product development at Purina.

The analysis of these recordings would become the foundation for Purina's Petivity Smart Litter Box Monitor, which, released in 2022, is already in more than 10,000 homes. The product is designed to alert pet owners when the measurements match the known patterns for certain cat ailments, and the team regularly updates the software to improve accuracy. The new paper documents the scientific steps behind its creation.

The monitor slides beneath an existing litter box and can recognize each cat in the house, according to the study. "Not only can we use their weight as a way to tell them apart but also their patterns in the litter box, the time of day they go and their normal habits to create what we call a 'paw print,' or signature, for that cat," McGowan says.

The team intends for the tool to communicate problems cats are having or offer reassurance to owners when all is well. Feline kidney disease, for example, a progressive illness that often goes unnoticed in early stages, can be treated if caught early. "By the time most pet owners would notice a behavioral change, the loss of renal function will be over 80 percent, and there's no turning back," McGowan says. According to Purina's website, although "information provided by Petivity Smart Litter Box Monitors is not intended to diagnose, treat, cure, or prevent any disease," the monitors can alert owners to "key changes that may indicate a health issue requiring a veterinary diagnosis."

Jessica Quimby, a small animal internal medicine specialist and professor at the Ohio State University, uses the Petivity monitor in her own research on feline kidney disease and recently published a paper showing clinically relevant results based on the monitor's measurements. (Quimby is a Nestlé Purina PetCare advisory board member.) "One of the very first things you might see with the onset of disease, even before we know the cat has kidney disease, is that they're losing weight and urinating more," Quimby says. "We can see those trends appearing on the Petivity data." Cats, she explains, are good at hiding health problems from their caregivers.

The smart litter box does, however, have its limitations. "If [cats] are close in weight and they have a similar pattern of elimination, that's a struggle for the system," says Langenfeld-McCoy. She recommends that five or fewer cats use one system. But improvements in AI capabilities should help distinguish between similar cats soon. "The deep-learning models can pick out subtle differences in behavior that maybe we don't even know exist, so we're moving towards that for those cats that are close in weight," she says.

Household antagonists–nudgy robot vacuums, percussive washing machines–can also cause confusion, so the team coached cat owners on placement during its research. But often when problems arise, the fix is less engineering than sociology. Langenfeld-McCoy recalls a home in which the AI indicated the cat had done its usual behavior but left nothing behind. "The family dog would come after the cat and have a snack, which was confusing the AI," she says. With a baby gate installed, the AI recovered its composure. Sometimes the outlier in the data is a Labrador.

Although the Petivity Smart Litter Box Monitor has been on the market for three years, the team waited until it had ample data to publish its scientific findings. "Smart" is one of those labels that arouses suspicion—smart toasters send overanxious notifications; smart fridges upsell milk. So when we hear "smart litter box," we picture an appliance with delusions of grandeur. The new study is a way for the team at Purina to pull back the curtain for users and skeptics alike and let cat owners determine whether "smart" gets to take off its quotation marks.

About the Author

Deni Ellis Béchard is Scientific American*'s senior writer for technology. He is author of 10 books and has received a Commonwealth Writers' Prize, a Midwest Book Award and a Nautilus Book Award for investigative journalism. He holds two master's degrees in literature, as well as a master's degree in biology from Harvard University. His most recent novel,* We Are Dreams in the Eternal Machine, *explores the ways that artificial intelligence could transform humanity. You can follow him on X, Instagram and Bluesky @denibechard*

Modern Rocketry Turns 100—and NASA Says the Best is Yet to Come

By Lee Billings

We are in the space age. Rockets launch to space almost every day. Orbital space stations have now housed humans continuously for decades. The sky is swarming with satellites and space telescopes. Humans have been to the moon—and are going back. And robots are scattered across the solar system and puttering around on the surface of Mars.

All of this incredible innovation owes a debt to a modest experiment that took place 100 years ago: On March 16, 1926, American physicist and engineer (and occasional *Scientific American* contributor) Robert H. Goddard launched an 11-foot-tall, 10-pound rocket prototype nicknamed "Nell" from a cabbage patch in Auburn, Mass. Nell was airborne for just a few seconds, but its flight was a milestone—the first-ever liftoff of a liquid-fueled rocket.

Before that moment among the cabbages, solid fuel was used in all previous rockets, dating all the way back to the gunpowder-filled "fire arrows" that were employed to fight invading Mongols in 13th-century China. Liquid fuels imbued rockets with a more powerful thrust and, thanks to their variable flow, also offered more control—precisely what would be needed for any serious attempt at spaceflight. Other early visionaries—Russia's Konstantin Tsiolkovsky and Germany's Hermann Oberth—had also realized the transformative potential of liquid-fueled rockets, but Goddard was the first to prove it.

The rest, as they say, is history. To commemorate the centenary of Goddard's flight and understand what the future holds for rocketry, *Scientific American* spoke with two NASA experts—Kurt Polzin, chief engineer of the Space Nuclear Propulsion Project at NASA's Marshall Space Flight Center, and David Manzella, senior technologist for in-space propulsion at NASA's Glenn Research Center.

[*An edited transcript of the interview follows.*]

Given how modest Goddard's "Nell" prototype was compared with today's rockets, do you think it's really accurate to say Nell's flight a century ago marks the beginning of "modern rocketry?"

KURT POLZIN: Robert Goddard was a pioneering figure who moved rocketry beyond its early roots in solid propellant systems, such as gunpowder-packed canisters. His scientific and analytical approach established a framework for systematically engineering and improving rocket components, a methodology still followed today.

Goddard's milestone flight laid the groundwork for the development of various space propulsion systems, including chemical rockets, nuclear-thermal rockets, and both solar- and nuclear-electric propulsion. Despite their differences, these systems share a common principle: converting a source of energy—whether chemical bonds, nuclear reactions or solar power—into a high-velocity stream of gas or particles that produces thrust.

Notably, Goddard's insight extended to electric propulsion. In his notes, he recognized the potential of accelerating charged particles, such as electrons, for propulsion—a concept that anticipated the ion thrusters now used in modern spacecraft.

Space launches are now so commonplace that they're scarcely seen as newsworthy. One might have the impression that we've reached the limit of what Goddard-inspired chemical rockets can do. What do you see as the remaining frontiers?

POLZIN: Chemical rockets, often associated with Goddard's pioneering work but now encompassing a century of collective innovation, have been the backbone of space exploration. Traditional propellant combinations such as liquid oxygen–liquid hydrogen, liquid oxygen–kerosene and various solid rocket motor propellants have been extensively refined. Recent developments from "new space" companies have introduced alternatives such as methane and hybrid propellants, which could offer further advantages in reliability, cost and operational flexibility.

Innovative approaches such as propulsive boost-stage landings (used by SpaceX's Falcon 9 and Blue Origin's New Glenn rockets, for instance) have reduced launch costs and increased launch frequency, making space more accessible than ever before. Chemical rockets will likely remain the primary means of reaching orbit for the foreseeable future, but it's important to remember no "ultimate" rocket can really exist—different missions require different solutions, and no single rocket design can serve every purpose.

Looking ahead, several frontiers remain for chemical rocketry. Advances in cryogenic fluid management may enable long-duration missions using chemical propellants by preventing boil-off, while continued work on nuclear propulsion and the proliferation of miniature propulsion systems for "CubeSats" and "SmallSats" promise to further expand the landscape. And we haven't even started to scratch the surface on use cases such as flying rockets on other planets, either to change locations or to boost payloads or astronauts off the surface.

David, this question is for you. In-space propulsion systems are rather different than rockets used to launch payloads from planets. What excites you about where rocketry is headed?

DAVID MANZELLA: Right, so I personally work on in-space propulsion systems, which are the technologies used to propel spacecraft once they reach orbit. For those systems, the fundamental challenge is not having a thrust-to-mass ratio of greater than 1; that is, they typically produce less thrust than would be required to lift a payload into orbit. But you need in-space propulsion because things placed in orbit are valuable, and you usually want to operate them for many years.

Currently that means, when you launch something, right from the start, you need to take all the fuel you'll need and use over that spacecraft's lifetime. The technologies we work on attempt to address this problem by making extremely fuel-efficient rocket engines—what we typically call thrusters—and one of the best ways to do that is to augment your propellant by adding electrical energy to it. And that energy is generated in space.

Today that's done using photovoltaic solar arrays. Keep in mind, though, that the more powerful those electrical systems are, the more oomph these electric propulsion thrusters can provide and the bigger the things we can push in space.

My favorite poster child for this is NASA's in-development Power and Propulsion Element, which has a 60-kilowatt power system that its onboard propulsion system could use to push an 18,000-kilogram spacecraft to the moon using less than 3,000 kg of propellant. Quite a contrast to launch vehicles, where 90 percent of the mass is propellant, right?

That's impressive. And I know the Power and Propulsion Element has yet to fly in space—you and your colleagues powered it up for the first time ever, in fact, in a test last year. What are you excited about further in the future?

MANZELLA: The exciting part of the future is that even higher-power systems can be developed, and photovoltaic solar arrays could one day be replaced with nuclear systems generating orders of magnitude more electricity. NASA is developing the technology to enable this for things that include the human exploration of Mars today. That's what excites me!

POLZIN: Let me jump in on this, too. What excites me most about the future of rocketry is the expanding horizon of both performance and application. Rockets, at their core, are tools—indispensable for enabling the exploration and utilization of space but not the instruments of discovery themselves. Their true value lies in their capacity to deliver the technologies and payloads that drive scientific investigation, exploration and, increasingly, the establishment of a lasting human presence beyond Earth.

On the performance front, innovation continues to push boundaries. Advances in propulsion systems promise greater efficiency, reliability and reach. This is realized through incremental improvements in chemical rockets, experimentation with new propellant combinations such as methane or hybrids or the pursuit of systems such as solar electric and nuclear propulsion. These developments are crucial for tackling ambitious missions, such as crewed journeys to Mars or deep-space sample return missions. And a diverse array of propulsion systems is essential to meet a broad spectrum of scientific, commercial and exploratory goals.

From the perspective of application, the most exciting developments involve moving beyond exploration to expansion and utilization. We are beginning to think boldly about questions like: How do we safely deliver and return humans from Mars? How can we collect and return samples from distant bodies in the solar system? What infrastructure is needed to transition from initial exploration to establishing a permanent presence in space? The vision extends further and involves leveraging resources and capabilities gained from expansion into space through NASA's Artemis program, enabling sustainable operations and new opportunities for science, industry and even daily life beyond our planet.

Ultimately, the future of rocketry is about empowering new possibilities. As end users gain access to a growing range of launch options, they are better equipped to pursue diverse missions: advancing scientific knowledge, developing commercial ventures or building the foundations of a permanent spacefaring civilization. The field thrives on bold thinking and inventive solutions, and I am most excited to see how these will shape the next era of space exploration and development.

MANZELLA: We are indeed entering a new age in the history of humankind where each and every one of us could be impacted by space-based systems daily. I think that trend will only accelerate in the future. It's clear that space is becoming an ever increasing part of our way of life as technology continues to advance. And yes, much of this progress traces back to Robert Goddard's first flight a century ago.

About the Author

Lee Billings is a science journalist specializing in astronomy, physics, planetary science, and spaceflight and is senior desk editor for physical science at Scientific American. *He is author of a critically acclaimed book,* Five Billion Years of Solitude: The Search for Life Among the Stars, *which in 2014 won a Science Communication Award from the American Institute of Physics. In addition to his work for* Scientific American, *Billings's writing has appeared in the* New York Times, *the* Wall Street Journal, *the* Boston Globe, Wired, New Scientist, Popular Science *and many other publications. Billings joined Scientific American in 2014 and previously worked as a staff editor at* SEED *magazine. He holds a B.A. in journalism from the University of Minnesota.*

Section 4: Engineering Marvels

This Engineer, Actor and Science Communicator Is Giving Science Its Rap

By Devin Williams

For many of us, the past year and a half may have seemed to slow way down. And in fact, some studies have shown just this. But Maynard Okereke's life has been anything but slow recently. He just got back from a month at sea where he worked with a team of oceanographers and roboticists to map the deep ocean and explore hydrothermal vents. That was right after he spent some time experiencing the sensation of weightlessness during a "zero gravity" flight with a group called Space for Humanity. And at the end of 2020 he even made an appearance on *Shark Tank* to co-pitch a "plant-based chicken." (The *nonchicken* chicken wowed the "sharks" and received venture funding.)

Okereke, better known as the "Hip Hop M.D.," is all hustle for science. Recently he (virtually) sat down with the Springer Nature Black Employee Network to discuss his background, accomplishments and current projects.

Okereke graduated from the University of Washington with a degree in civil engineering. He remembers growing up as "one of very few minorities" in his classes. These experiences became more prevalent as he became older and moved into the workspace. "Going into my job as a lead engineer and walking into a room and people not believing I was the lead scientist or engineer..., having those experiences while I was working professionally really impacted me and was always something that stood front and center," he says.

Okereke started a platform called Hip Hop Science with the goal of encouraging people from minority groups and youth to pursue more advanced career paths. He uses the avenues of music, entertainment and comedy as tools to educate on a wide variety of subjects with a style that he describes as "Bill Nye meets Worldstar."

This discussion is part of a speaker series hosted by the Black Employee Network at Springer Nature, the publisher of *Scientific American*. The series aims to highlight Black contributions to STEM (science, technology, engineering and mathematics)—a history that has not been widely recognized. It will cover career paths, role models and mentorship, and diversity in STEM.

New Glasses Can Transcribe Speech in Real Time

By O. Rose Broderick

When Paul Shuttleworth bought himself a very expensive pair of eyeglasses for Christmas last year, it was a peculiar gift. The glasses didn't improve his eyesight, weren't particularly stylish and uncomfortably pressed down on his nose.

But these glasses are a vital tool for him.

Shuttleworth, age 40, a resident of Manchester, England, is profoundly deaf in both ears and uses a mobile live audio transcription app as his main conversational tool. But the glasses have helped him talk and participate in conversations in ways that he had never been able to before. These fancy shades automatically transcribe the words someone is saying and display the text as subtitles on the lenses in front of his eyes.

The buzz is building for such "live-captioning glasses," and a slew of companies have rolled out their own versions in the past few years. These high-tech glasses have the potential to help people who are deaf or hard of hearing communicate more seamlessly with hearing people. But they aren't perfect, and they may never fully replace human translators.

In July Tom Pritsky, co-founder of TranscribeGlass, put out a TikTok video that demonstrated his company's live-captioning glasses providing subtitles for words that he spoke, and it went viral.These glasses are not just a technological fad for Pritsky, who has moderate to severe bilateral hearing loss. They actively improve his quality of life and ability to converse with people. "It helps me fill in the blanks," says Pritsky, a graduate student in biomedical informatics at Stanford University. He also wears hearing aids. "The hearing aids give me audio, but it's unclear, and I miss words," Pritsky says. "If I can fill in some of those words via captions and subtitles, then it helps me continue to understand the conversation and not lose the thread."

Live-captioning glasses are now starting to hit the market, thanks to improvements in speech recognition technology and battery life. Nearly 2.5 billion people are projected to have some kind of hearing loss by 2050. Experts say that older people with hearing loss are the most likely to benefit from these glasses. Many older people need hearing aids but do not wear them because of stigma and difficulty adapting to the technology. Live-captioning glasses often resemble regular glasses, which are already more normalized in society than hearing aids are.

Giving older people with age-related hearing loss access to live captioning may improve their social relationship with family and friends, says Thad Starner, a computer science professor at the Georgia Institute of Technology. In the early 2010s Starner helped develop Google Glass, a now discontinued device resembling eyeglasses that projected information on a tiny prism in front of the wearer's eye.

A Game-Changer

Real-time captioning is not a totally new technology. People who are deaf or hard of hearing routinely use apps such as Otter to transcribe a conversation as they're having it. But having to ping-pong between the person they're talking with and their phone can be frustrating and exhausting. Having captions in your field of vision is a game changer, Pritsky says.

Most live-captioning glasses are composed of the glasses themselves, a tiny microphone, an onboard computer that processes speech, a battery and some way to display text. Some glasses contain all of these components, whereas other devices sit on top of a regular pair of glasses. Improvements in speech recognition software have really enabled these technological advances, says Dan Scarfe, CEO of XRAI Glass, a company that makes a speech-processing app that can be used with an array of live-captioning glasses. "I don't think we're more than six months away from a killer piece of hardware that you can absolutely use for this. Then it's just a question of finding people who want to use it," he says.

Despite the media buzz, a relatively modest number of live-captioning glasses have been sold. Scarfe says more than 5,000 people are part of XRAI Glass's pilot program, and Pritsky says "thousands" have ordered TranscribeGlass.

Nevertheless, these sales represent a significant step forward for the technology, says Starner, who has been a part of the field since its infancy. Starner, a wearable computing aficionado, has been wearing some kind of head-mounted display almost every day for 30 years. "It used to be that in order to have a head-borne display that had any sort of battery life, you ended up carrying around seven pounds of lead weight with you," says Starner, who used to carry a battery in a shoulder bag. "Literally, my first battery was a motorcycle battery."

Starner has seen a lot of technological failures during the past three decades. But now he believes that the current crop has promise and that live-captioning glasses will soon be a normalized, household technology because of more portable batteries and speech recognition upgrades. For this to happen, society's attitudes toward the glasses must continue to shift. The devices need to become unremarkable, he says. "Suppose I walk up to somebody at the airport, and I ask, 'Can I get directions to the bathroom?' And the person says, 'Oh, is that the new Apple head-borne display?' What you really want to do is get to the bathroom. You want the conversation to be about the conversation, not about the technology," Starner says.

An Important but Imperfect Tool

While live-captioning glasses could be an incredibly powerful tool for millions of people, they are not a complete solution. For many people with hearing loss, understanding a hearing friend in a crowded restaurant is a nightmare. Similarly, live-captioning software struggles to capture accurate conversation in these spaces. Background noise remains a thorny issue that these glasses do not yet fully solve.

Many people who are deaf or hard of hearing are excited by this technology, but some see it as a threat to requests for sign language interpreters. Captions do not display a speaker's identity, emotions or inflections; interpreters can convey all of that context.

These glasses also place the burden of communication on the people using them—expectations that Deaf people are tired of having to meet, says Raja Kushalnagar, a professor and director of the Information Technology program at Gallaudet University. "The hearing person might think that, you know, 'What's wrong with you? What's wrong with the glasses?'" he says. "They think it's not the tools but the [Deaf people] themselves who are the problem."

These glasses are mainly a tool to interface with the larger hearing public—Deaf communities that primarily use sign language have no need for them. But Kushalnagar has already seen the technology's impact on his everyday life when conversing with his hearing son. "Say I'm cooking now—chopping vegetables or something in the kitchen. I'll be able to read the captions while I'm still cutting," he says. "I would never have been able to have that conversation with my son before like that. Now I can walk, and I can speak with my son at the same time."

When Shuttleworth took a test a few years ago to become an IT technician, he passed with distinction because he had been given resources necessary for him to understand the information. Shuttleworth now uses his glasses alongside his mobile app at his job. He desperately wishes he had been given access to these tools growing up, tools that could have changed his whole life's trajectory. "If I had that mobile app and the glasses, I wouldn't be sitting here talking to you now," he says.

About the Author

O. Rose Broderick is a freelance science journalist and former news intern at Scientific American *whose work focuses on energy, disability and disaster. Follow Broderick on Bluesky.*

Section 5: Mathematics

3 Revolutionary Women of Mathematics

By Avery Carr

From the profound revelations of the shape of space to the furthest explorations reachable by imagination and logic, the history of mathematics has always been seen as a masculine endeavor. Names like Gauss, Euler, Riemann, Poincare, Erdős, and the more modern Wiles, Tao, Perelman, and Zhang, all of them associated with the most beautiful mathematics discovered since the dawn of humanity, are all men. The book Men of Mathematics, written by E.T. Bell in 1937, is just one example of how this "fact" has been reinforced in in the public consciousness.

Even today, it is no secret that male mathematicians still dominate the field. But this should not distract us from the revolutionary contributions women have made. We have notable women to thank for modern computation, revelations on the geometry of space, cornerstones of abstract algebra, and major advances in decision theory, number theory, and celestial mechanics that continue to provide crucial breakthroughs in applied areas like cryptography, computer science, and physics.

The works of geniuses like Julia Robinson on Hilbert's Tenth Problem in number theory, Emmy Noether in abstract algebra and physics, and Ada Lovelace in computer science, are just three examples of women whose contributions have been absolutely essential.

Julia Robinson (1919-1985)

At the turn of the twentieth century the famed German mathematician David Hilbert published a set of twenty-three tantalizing problems that had evaded the most brilliant of mathematical minds. Among them was his tenth problem, which asked if a general algorithm could be constructed to determine the solvability of any Diophantine equation (those polynomial equations with only integer coefficients and integer solutions). Imagine, for any Diophantine equation of the infinite set of such equations a machine that can tell whether it can be solved. Mathematicians often deal with infinite questions of this nature that exist far beyond resolution by simple extensive observations. This particular problem drew the attention of a Berkeley mathematician named Julia Robinson. Over several decades, Robinson collaborated with colleagues including Martin Davis and Hillary Putnam that resulted in formulating a condition that would answer Hilbert's question in the negative.

In 1970 a young Russian mathematician named Yuri Matiyasevich solved the problem using the insight provided by Robinson, Davis, and Putnam. With her brilliant contributions in number theory, Robinson was a remarkable mathematician who paved the way to answering one of the greatest pure math questions ever proposed. In a Mathematical Association of America article, "The Autobiography of Julia Robinson", her sister and biographer Constance Read wrote, "She herself, in the normal course of events, would never have considered recounting the story of her own life. As far as she was concerned, what she had done mathematically was all that was significant."

Emmy Noether (1882-1935)

Sitting in an abstract math course for any length of time, one is bound to hear the name Emmy Noether. Her notable work spans subjects from physics to modern algebra, making Noether one of the most important figures in mathematical history. Her 1913 result on the calculus of variations, leading to Noether's Theorem is considered one of the most important theorems in mathematics—and one that shaped modern physics. Noether's theory of ideals and commutative rings forms a foundation for any researcher in the field of higher algebra.

The influence of her work continues to shine as a beacon of intuition for those who grapple with understanding physical reality more abstractly. Mathematicians and physicists alike admire her epoch contributions that provide deep insights within their respective disciplines. In 1935, Albert Einstein wrote in a letter to the New York Times, "In the judgment of the most competent living mathematicians, Fräulein Noether was the most significant creative mathematical genius thus far produced since the higher education of women began."

Ada Lovelace (1815-1852)

In 1842, Cambridge mathematics professor Charles Babbage gave a lecture at the University of Turin on the design of his Analytical Engine (the first computer). Mathematician Luigi Menabrea later transcribed the notes of that lecture to French. The young Countess Ada Lovelace was commissioned by Charles Wheatstone (a friend of Babbage) to translate the notes of Menabrea into English. She is known as the "world's first programmer" due to her insightful augmentation of that transcript. Published in 1843, Lovelace added her own notes including Section G, which outlined an algorithm to calculate Bernoulli numbers. In essence, she took Babbage's theoretical engine and made it a computational reality. Lovelace provided a path for others to shed light on the mysteries of computation that continues to impact technology.

Despite their profound contributions, the discoveries made by these three women are often overshadowed by the contributions of their male counterparts. According to a 2015 United Nations estimate, the number of men and women in the world is almost equal (101.8 men for every 100 women). One could heuristically argue, therefore that we should see roughly the same number of women as men working in the field of mathematics.

One large reason that we don't is due to our failure to recognize the historical accomplishments of female mathematicians. Given the crucial role of science and technology in the modern world, however, it is imperative as a civilization to promote and encourage more women to pursue careers in mathematics.

About the Author

Avery Carr is a senior analyst and past senior editor for the American Mathematical Society Grad Blog. He and his wife, Alison, live in Olive Branch, MS.

Mathematicians Crack a Fractal Conjecture on Chaos

By Lyndie Chiou

The world may seem orderly, but randomness and chaos shape everything in the universe, from enormous galaxies all the way down to subatomic particles. Take a chilly window sheeting over with ice: even one oddly shaped snowflake can exert an influence on the final frosty pattern.

Understanding how random fluctuations can ripple out to produce global effects is what French mathematician Vincent Vargas of the University of Geneva in Switzerland set out to do more than 10 years ago. His earliest ideas for simple geometries appeared in a decade-old paper, but it wasn't until 2023, while he was working with Christophe Garban of the University of Lyon in France, that the concept finally crystallized into what is now known as the Garban-Vargas conjecture. Now mathematicians have proved the conjecture using an insightful technique that should open the door for understanding much more complex systems.

The conjecture involves the behavior of a form of randomness found in a huge range of fields, from quantum chaos to Brownian motion to air turbulence. Mathematicians use a mathematical "measuring tape" called Gaussian multiplicative chaos, or GMC, to pick out subtle patterns hidden inside an otherwise impenetrable sea of randomness. GMC has even been used to find patterns in the prime numbers. The topic is one of the most important and fundamental ideas in probability theory today.

French mathematician Jean-Pierre Kahane is credited with first developing GMC in 1985, although his pioneering work was quickly forgotten. "I was one of the people who revived his work," Vargas says. "I met him many times, and he said he was amazed how important the topic [had] become. Everywhere on the planet, people are working on something related to Gaussian chaos."

Vargas first encountered the measure while studying turbulence and finance. He then came across it again in a project on conformal field theory, which is used to study patterns that remain constant as you zoom in or out. Lately he has focused on investigating its fundamental mathematical nature.

To understand GMC, imagine a turbulent fluid full of swirling eddies at many different scales. Enormous eddies randomly break apart into smaller ones, which themselves break into even smaller eddies, in a vast, nested hierarchy of randomness. GMC serves as a mathematical model that measures this kind of multiscale randomness–it captures random fluctuations that persist across every scale of the observation. Because of this, it is often referred to as a fractal measure.

Mathematicians have uncovered surprising behaviors in the types of randomness governed by GMC. For instance, events at the smallest scales can govern the entire system; the powerful tendrils of fractal structure shape chaos at every level. As a result, these systems cannot be understood by looking at averages. Instead the rules of GMC produce a universal picture that applies to every scale.

But this fascinating picture only holds up to a critical threshold. If the underlying randomness becomes too strong, the GMC measure collapses. Or, in the language of eddies, once enough randomness infuses the swirls, they become unstable, losing all their hidden order. Like ice transitioning to a liquid, this breakdown marks an important phase transition for chaos.

In 2023 Garban and Vargas introduced a new lens for studying GMC chaos. It came from a field of mathematics called harmonic analysis. Instead of looking at eddies directly, they examined the frequencies of patterns hidden in the eddies, much like analyzing a complex sound by breaking it into pure tones.

Then an idea came to them. If they could match two completely different physical descriptions–complexity and harmonics–

they might learn something new. Mathematicians refer to this idea of matching unrelated physical descriptions as matching "dimensions."

As an example, consider snowflakes falling to the ground. As the snow gently lands, two possible dimensions might be how many patterns appear in the distribution of the snowflakes and how many clumpy piles form across different scales. But is there a formula that can relate the two dimensions of patterns (harmonics) and clumpiness (correlations)?

"The key word is dimension," Vargas says. "That's the name of the game. You have lots of natural dimensions, but when do they coincide?"

After studying systems governed by GMC on a circle, the duo conjectured an extraordinarily elegant equation that matched a GMC system's correlation dimension to its harmonic dimension.

Unfortunately they couldn't prove their formula, even for a simple geometry. In 2023 they posted their conjecture to the preprint server arXiv.org, and it subsequently became a major open problem.

In 2024 mathematicians Zhaofeng Lin and Yanqi Qiu of the Hangzhou Institute for Advanced Study, University of Chinese Academy of Sciences, and Mingjie Tan of Wuhan University resolved the conjecture. Their research, which was posted as a preprint to arXiv.org and has not yet been peer-reviewed, not only confirmed the formula but also revealed *why* it works.

Mathematically, they likened GMC to a "fair betting game," in which the expected winnings remain constant no matter the size of the game. When applied to fractal fluctuations, this means that the system remains balanced as you zoom in and out, and each smaller scale contributes randomness in a way that conserves energy.

Mathematicians call a process that exhibits this type of fair, scale-by-scale behavior a martingale. Unlike normal betting games, however, chaos "games" are much more complex, requiring higher-dimensional martingales.

"I heard about this conjecture during an online math workshop," Qiu says. "I had focused on martingales for my Ph.D. thesis a few years back, and I had a hunch they would be the right tool here."

The group used its higher-dimensional martingale structure to carefully track the accumulation of randomness at every scale. And sure enough, by conserving energy, numerous tiny "fair games" combined to give the same formula for the decay that Garban and Vargas had conjectured.

Qiu and his colleagues' proof not only settled the conjecture but also paved the way for further proofs on more complex fractal models. The roadway to a complete theory isn't entirely free of barriers, though. Even the new method fails when randomness forces the system to its critical phase-transition point. This phase transition itself is a rich and intriguing topic with its own set of deep questions, mathematicians say. But "to go further," Qiu says, "we need new ideas."

About the Author

Lyndie Chiou is a scientist, a science writer and founder of ZeroDivZero, a science conference website. Her writing has also appeared in Sky & Telescope. Follow her on X @lyndie_chiou

How the World's Most Famous Code Was Cracked

By Jack Murtagh

The 35-year-old saga of *Kryptos*, an enigmatic sculpture containing four encrypted messages outside the headquarters of the U.S. Central Intelligence Agency, recently took a bizarre twist. Cryptographers had broken the first three passages in the 1990s, just a few years after artist Jim Sanborn erected the copper structure. But the fourth, known as K4, remained a 97-character fortress—that is, until last September, when journalists Jarett Kobek and Richard Byrne discovered the answer in the Smithsonian archives.

How does one crack the world's most famous code? The breakthroughs on *Kryptos* provide a guided tour of the cat-and-mouse game played by code makers and code breakers that has defined information security for millennia.

The core challenge of cryptography is to deliver a secret message securely in the presence of eavesdroppers. The strategy always involves the same ingredients: The message, called the plaintext, gets distorted (the encryption) so that anybody who intercepts it sees only garbled gibberish (the ciphertext). Ideally, only those with a secret key can decrypt it. If you share your secret key with the intended recipient and nobody else, then you can, in theory, communicate with them in code. Cryptography underlies everyday financial transactions and online communication, not just spy messages.

To understand *Kryptos*, we'll need to dig into early cryptosystems and why they failed. One of the simplest and oldest encryption methods dates back to a historical secret keeper: Julius Caesar. The Caesar cipher obscures messages by shifting every letter of the alphabet by some fixed amount. Here the key is a number between 1 and 25. Say we pick 5; the encryption of "hello" would be "mjqqt" because M is five letters after H, J is five letters after E, and so on. (If you reach the end of the alphabet, then wrap back around to the beginning.) In a more entertaining example, astute fans of the 1968 film *2001: A Space Odyssey* have noticed that the name of the rogue artificial intelligence called HAL is "IBM" with a Caesar-cipher shift of one letter backward. (Director Stanley Kubrick insisted that it was a coincidence.) Although Caesar trusted this method for his confidential correspondence, it's a lousy way to protect state secrets. If an adversary learns that you encrypt messages with a Caesar cipher, they need to try only 25 different keys to recover the original text.

A substitution cipher offers the most natural upgrade. Instead of merely shifting the alphabet, you scramble it. The letter A might become Q, B might become X, C might become D, and so on, with no consistent order. This *seems* far more secure. A Caesar cipher has only 25 possible keys, but a full substitution cipher has 403,291,461,126,605,635,584,000,000. (There are 26 factorial ways to mix up the alphabet, or 26 × 25 × 24 × 23 ... 3 × 2 × 1.) A brute-force search to check every key isn't feasible, yet substitution ciphers are still woefully insecure by today's standards. If you don't already know why, ask yourself how you would go about decoding a page of text encrypted in this way.

The flaw in a substitution cipher is that it leaves patterns in language intact. English has a distinct fingerprint. E accounts for more than 12 percent of all letters in English text, whereas Z crops up less than 0.1 percent of the time. If you intercept a page of gibberish encrypted with a substitution cipher and see that the letter J appears more often than any other letter, it's a good bet that J stands for E. The second most common letter is probably T. Furthermore, single letters almost certainly stand for A or I (the only frequently used one-letter English words), and common two- and three-letter words can give code breakers a foot in the door as well. Known as frequency analysis, this method is the subject of popular newspaper puzzles called cryptograms; it also played a critical role in deciphering the first three *Kryptos* passages.

To encrypt the first two *Kryptos* messages, K1 and K2–which contain 63 and 372 characters, respectively–Sanborn used the next level up: the Vigenère cipher. Invented in the 16th century and named after French cryptographer Blaise de Vigenère, it stood unbroken for 300 years, earning it the nickname "*le chiffre indéchiffrable*" (the indecipherable cipher). It works by applying several different Caesar ciphers to a single plaintext. For example, maybe we shift the first letter of the message forward by 19, the second letter forward by 16, the third letter forward by 25 and then repeat. (The fourth letter shifts by 19, the fifth by 16, the sixth by 25, and so on.) These shift amounts constitute the key, which is typically represented by a word corresponding to those locations in the alphabet. In this case, the key is SPY because S, P and Y are, respectively, the 19th, 16th and 25th letters.

The Vigenère cipher ingeniously defeats straightforward frequency analysis because not all E's, for example, will get mapped to the same letter. Imagine that the first two letters of a message are both E. We would shift the first by 19 to an X and the second by 16 to a U. But clever cryptanalysts can still break through. If you can guess the length of the key (for example, three for SPY), you can break the problem apart. You take the ciphertext's first, fourth, seventh and 10th letters, and so on, then put them in a pile. All of them were shifted according to the same key letter: S. Now you can conduct frequency analysis on just that pile. You do the same for all the letters shifted according to P: the second, fifth, eighth, and so on. The "unbreakable" cipher becomes three simple Caesar ciphers. Not sure of the length of the key? Careful scrutiny of the ciphertext can sometimes provide clues, but if all else fails, try all possible lengths. Too time-consuming? A computer program can help with the search.

Sanborn encrypted K1 and K2 with the keys "PALIMPSEST" and "ABSCISSA," respectively. The former, a poetic choice, refers to an object on which writing has been erased and something new has been written over it multiple times. An abscissa is the x value of an (x, y) coordinate pair. As is common practice in Vigenère ciphers, Sanborn also used a modified alphabet for the shifting: in this case, KRYPTOSABCDEFGHIJLMNQUVWXZ, which he etched into the sculpture.

Sanborn switched methods for K3, a 337-character ciphertext. Here he chose a transposition cipher in which he jumbled the letters in the message as though it were a massive anagram. The jumble in this type of cipher typically follows certain rules so that an intended recipient with a key can easily restore the letters to their rightful order. Cryptographers quickly suspected that K3 used this cipher. Why? You guessed it–frequency analysis. The letter distribution in the ciphertext matched what would be expected in typical English text, suggesting that letters had been shuffled, not substituted.

At least three independent efforts deciphered the first three *Kryptos* messages. Computer scientist Jim Gillogly announced that he had broken them with the aid of a computer in 1999. Only *then* did the CIA reveal that one of its analysts, David Stein, had solved all three by hand in 1998. And only then did the National Security Agency advertise that a small internal team had conquered them way back in 1992.

K4 resisted all attempts for 35 years. Perhaps Sanborn intentionally cranked up its complexity to reflect the strides made in cryptographic science since the days of Vigenère. Breaking full-fledged modern cryptography would amount to not merely a cleverer deployment of frequency analysis but a revolution in our understanding of math itself. That's because cutting-edge encryption shrouds information behind mathematical problems (such as factoring enormous numbers) that are conjectured to be unsolvable in any practical amount of time. To break the encryption, one would have to find a fast solution to these supposedly insurmountable problems, an act that would overturn a foundational assumption of modern math.

This past fall Sanborn was planning to auction off the solution to K4—an encrypted message that starts with "OBKR"—to relieve himself of the role of sole steward of its secrets. The auction announcement referenced original "coding charts" at the Smithsonian Institution. Rather than actually deciphering K4, journalists Kobek and Byrne requested access to the documents and found scraps of paper containing K4's plaintext. On September 3, 2025, the duo e-mailed Sanborn with the solution.

Journalists uncovering the answer to K4 in the Smithsonian archives perfectly exemplifies how hackers infiltrate 21st-century cryptography: through side doors. To the best of anyone's knowledge, the modern encryption that protects your e-mails and credit card purchases, when implemented correctly, works. Data breaches are rarely the result of hackers breaking an encryption; rather people find some other weak link in the security chain. They run phishing scams to trick people into disclosing their log-in credentials. They exploit a bug in a website's code. That is, they target the flawed, forgetful and disorganized humans who use encryption. The discovery of K4's plaintext was akin to finding somebody's password scribbled on a sticky note in their office. Some find this climax disappointing, but we could also view it as a metaphor befitting of an art piece meant to honor cryptography through the ages.

The artist doesn't seem to share this perspective: Sanborn asked the journalists to sign nondisclosure agreements. (They refused but agreed to keep the plaintext a secret.) Those still longing for a puzzle are in luck because the public doesn't know what K4 says or how it was encrypted. Nobody fully understands the enigmatic messages that K1–K3 revealed. Sanborn also confirmed the existence of a K5 in an open letter published last August. Code breakers have plenty to look forward to in the next era of *Kryptos*.

About the Author

Jack Murtagh is a freelance math writer and puzzle creator. He writes a column on mathematical curiosities for Scientific American *and creates daily puzzles for the Morning Brew newsletter. He holds a Ph.D. in theoretical computer science from Harvard University. Follow him on X @JackPMurtagh*

How Teen Mathematician Hannah Cairo Disproved a Major Mathematical Wave Conjecture

By Emma R. Hasson

When Hannah Cairo was 17 years old, she disproved the Mizohata-Takeuchi conjecture, a long-standing guess in the field of harmonic analysis about how waves behave on curved surfaces. The conjecture was posed in the 1980s, and mathematicians had been trying to prove it ever since. If the Mizohata-Takeuchi conjecture turned out to be true, it would illuminate many other significant questions in the field. But after hitting wall after wall trying to prove it, Cairo managed to come up with a counterexample: a circumstance where the waves don't behave as predicted by the conjecture. Therefore, the conjecture can't be true.

Cairo got hooked on the problem after being assigned a simpler version of the conjecture to prove as a homework assignment for a class she was taking at the University of California, Berkeley. "It took me a while to convince [course instructor] Ruixiang Zhang that my proposal was actually correct," she says. Now, under Zhang's advisement, she has a paper on the preprint server arXiv.org and was invited to present her results at the International Conference on Harmonic Analysis and Partial Differential Equations in El Escorial, Spain.

Cairo says she loves talking about her research and giving presentations with colorful and descriptive slides. When asked what she studies, Cairo says, in short, "points, lines and waves."

Born and raised in the Bahamas, Cairo moved to California at the age of 16, where she began to take classes at U.C. Berkeley. Now, at 18 years old, she is on to a Ph.D. program at the University of Maryland to continue her research in Fourier restriction theory. Cairo has faced many difficulties in her journey, but she has found comfort and belonging in the field of mathematics and in the work itself.

Scientific American spoke to Cairo about the way harmonic analysis is like dropping stones into a still pond, her transgender identity and the reasons she loves mathematics.

[*An edited transcript of the interview follows.*]

Beyond "points, lines, and waves," how would you explain your field of study, harmonic analysis?

Imagine that you're at a pond, and it's a very still pond, and you drop a stone into it. You see these circular waves spreading out.

If you drop two stones in the pond, then you might notice this pattern called an interference pattern: instead of looking like circles, they overlap. You get high points, low points. And you get these interesting shapes [where they intersect]. What if you were to use a whole bunch of ripples–then what would you get? In harmonic analysis, you can actually prove that if you drop your stones in the right place in the pond, you can get any shape that you want.

My specialty is known as Fourier restriction theory, which is the subdiscipline of harmonic analysis that I work in, where we ask what kind of objects can we build if we're only allowed to use certain kinds of waves. What if we're only allowed to drop the stones in certain parts of the pond? You won't be able to get just any object. In fact, you're only going to be able to get a relatively small family of objects. What the Mizohata-Takeuchi conjecture says is that the shape of the objects that we get are concentrated along lines.

What does it mean to be "concentrated along lines"?

One way to think of the shape of objects is to ask: What is curvature? There are a few different ways you can define it. One possible way is to take a thin, long rectangle and ask how much of your circle can lie in this thin rectangle. What you'll find is that not very much of it can because it bends away, right? On the other hand, if you take something flat like the edge of a square, then you can get a whole side of that square just on one thin tube. So that means that the square is not as "curved" as a circle.

For the Mizohata-Takeuchi conjecture, we say, consider this object that we're building out of these waves. And we want to say that not very much is going to lie on shapes that do not contain very many lines or thin rectangles.

So how did you manage to disprove this conjecture?

I looked at these shapes, and one thing that I realized is that the specific kind of waves that are used are concentrated along thick rectangles. This is actually something that is well known. So you end up looking at these waves that are concentrated on rectangles: You take these waves, and they intersect each other, and they make these certain shapes, but here [instead of circle waves] we use rectangle waves. So then we have all of these rectangle waves meeting each other. What I realized is that the shape of where they meet is not quite at the right angle to agree with the direction that these rectangles are pointing in. And so this led me to a rather complicated construction using fractals to arrange these rectangles.

The original fractal construction doesn't actually show up in your paper though. What was your final counterexample?

What I found out is that if you arrange these waves by taking a high-dimensional hypercube and projecting it down into smaller-dimensional space and then taking only those waves that lie in your region, then this is how you can determine where to put them [to break the conjecture].

What first got you interested in math?

I've always been interested in math. I think that, for me, mathematics is an art. In my childhood, I was somewhat lonely. Math was sort of there as a friend almost. I think that art cannot necessarily be a friend in every way that a friend can be, but I think art is like a friend. And so, for as long as I can remember, I've always loved mathematics.

Tell me more about how math was a friend to you. I think a lot of people don't think of math as very friendly.

There's an analogy that I like to make, which is to another form of art: painting. And I think that if one were to take a class on paint, you could memorize the dates and times at which various forms of paint were developed—and maybe even which paints were used by which painters. And then you can figure out what processes you can use to determine what type of paint it is. I imagine this is useful in art history, but this is not art.... I shouldn't say that. Maybe there is an art to learning about paint. I'm not going to claim that there isn't because I don't study paint. But I think that math is a little bit like that—in school, people learn about [the mathematical version of] paint; they're not learning about painting.

Mathematics is comforting to me because it's a way of exploring—to explore ideas and to think about them and to build more ideas out of other ideas. What's comforting about that is that it's independent of the world in some ways. If I'm having a sad day, a happy day, if I move to Maryland (I did just move to Maryland), mathematics is still there, and it is still the same thing. It's also just something that can occupy my mind.

You've mentioned to me that you're transgender. How has that affected your journey?

I think that it's probably more relevant in my journey as a person than as a mathematician. Being trans has forced me to see things about the world that I maybe otherwise wouldn't have seen. It's made me see the world differently and made me see people differently and made me see myself differently.

Fortunately, in the math community, I think that most mathematicians are fine with trans people. I think that it used to be more significant [in my day to day] than it is now. These days it doesn't really make much of a difference.

Why have you decided to go on the record now as being trans?
Trans visibility is important. People have ideas about who trans people are, and I think that it's best to broaden that. Maybe I'm also hoping that people who think that trans people are "less" than cisgender people might find themselves questioning that.

The other thing is that it's good for trans people to know that they're not alone. I think that part of what helps trans people realize that they're trans is to know that there are more options for who you can be as a trans person. That's important to me.

Thank you so much for sharing that. Where is your favorite place to do math?
If I'm trying to be productive in writing something down, then I like to be at my desk, and I like to listen to Bach. If I am just trying to think about ideas, then my favorite place to do that is somewhere where I don't have to pay attention to very much else. I could just be sitting down somewhere thinking about stuff, or I could be going for a walk outside.

I also like to talk to other people about math, which is another kind of doing math. I really like to give presentations about mathematics. I have these handwritten slides with all these colors and drawings. Luckily, in harmonic analysis, I can give a presentation like this, and then everybody is so happy, and they tell me my slides are cute.

What's next for your research?
I'm working on a research project with my adviser on Mizohata-Takeuchi and adjacent stuff and about a sort of different thing: the local Mizohata-Takeuchi conjecture.

The process of learning more about this kind of mathematics is pretty exciting—not just for me learning more about what's out there but for the math community as a whole to try to understand these kinds of things better. [That's] something that I'm excited about.

About the Author

Emma R. Hasson is Scientific American's *Games ace and a Ph.D. candidate in mathematics at the City University of New York Graduate Center with expertise in math education and communication. Hasson was also a 2025 AAAS Mass Media Fellow at* Scientific American.

Mathematicians Crack 125-Year-Old Problem, Unite Three Physics Theories

By Jack Murtagh

When the greatest mathematician alive unveils a vision for the next century of research, the math world takes note. That's exactly what happened in 1900 at the International Congress of Mathematicians at Sorbonne University in Paris. Legendary mathematician David Hilbert presented 10 unsolved problems as ambitious guideposts for the 20th century. He later expanded his list to include 23 problems, and their influence on mathematical thought over the past 125 years cannot be overstated.

Hilbert's sixth problem was one of the loftiest. He called for "axiomatizing" physics, or determining the bare minimum of mathematical assumptions behind all its theories. Broadly construed, it's not clear whether mathematical physicists could ever be sure they had fully met this challenge. Hilbert mentioned some specific subgoals, however, and researchers have since refined his vision into concrete steps toward its solution.

In March 2025 mathematicians Yu Deng of the University of Chicago and Zaher Hani and Xiao Ma, both at the University of Michigan, posted a paper to the preprint server arXiv.org in which they claim to have achieved one of these goals. If their work withstands scrutiny, it will mark a major stride toward grounding physics in math and may open the door to analogous breakthroughs in other areas of physics.

In the paper, the researchers suggest they have figured out how to unify three physical theories that explain the motion of fluids. These theories govern a range of engineering applications from aircraft design to weather prediction—but until now, they rested on assumptions that hadn't been rigorously proven. This breakthrough won't change the theories themselves, but it mathematically justifies them and strengthens our confidence that the equations work the way we think they do.

Each theory differs in how much it zooms in on a flowing liquid or gas. At the microscopic level, fluids are composed of particles–little billiard balls bopping around and occasionally colliding–and Newton's laws of motion work well to describe their trajectories.

But when you zoom out to consider the collective behavior of vast numbers of particles, at the so-called mesoscopic level, it's no longer convenient to model each one individually. In 1872 Austrian theoretical physicist Ludwig Boltzmann addressed this problem when he developed (what became known as) the Boltzmann equation. Instead of tracking the behavior of every particle, the equation considers the likely behavior of a typical particle. This statistical perspective smooths over the low-level details in favor of higher-level trends. The equation allows physicists to calculate the evolution of quantities such as momentum and thermal conductivity in the fluid without painstakingly considering every microscopic collision.

Zoom out further, and you find yourself in the macroscopic world. Here we view a fluid not as a collection of discrete particles but as a single continuous substance. At this level of analysis, a different suite of equations–the Euler and Navier-Stokes equations–accurately describe how fluids move and how their physical properties interrelate without recourse to particles at all.

The three levels of analysis all describe the same underlying reality–how fluids flow. In principle, each theory should build on the theory below it in the hierarchy: at the macroscopic level, the Euler and Navier-Stokes equations should follow logically from the Boltzmann equation at the mesoscopic level, which in turn should follow logically from Newton's laws of motion at the microscopic level. This relation is the kind of axiomatization that Hilbert called for in his sixth problem, and he explicitly referenced Boltzmann's work on gases in his write-up of the problem. We expect complete theories of physics to follow mathematical rules that explain a phenomenon from the microscopic to the macroscopic levels. If scientists fail to bridge that gap, then it might suggest a misunderstanding in our existing theories.

Unifying the three perspectives on fluid dynamics has been a stubborn challenge for the field, but Deng, Hani and Ma might have just done it. Their achievement builds on decades of incremental progress. Prior advancements all came with some kind of asterisk, though; for example, the derivations involved worked only on short timescales, in a vacuum, or under other simplifying conditions.

The new proof broadly consists of three steps: derive the macroscopic theory from the mesoscopic one, derive the mesoscopic theory from the microscopic one, and then stitch them together in a single derivation of the macroscopic laws all the way from the microscopic ones.

The first step was previously understood, and even Hilbert himself contributed to it. Deriving the mesoscopic from the microscopic, however, has been much more mathematically difficult. Remember, the mesoscopic setting is about the collective behavior of vast numbers of particles. So Deng, Hani and Ma looked at what happens to Newton's equations as the number of individual particles colliding and ricocheting grows to infinity and the particles' size shrinks to zero. They proved that when you stretch Newton's equations to these extremes, the statistical behavior of the system—or the likely behavior of a typical particle in the fluid—converges to the solution of the Boltzmann equation. This step forms a bridge by enabling one to derive the mesoscopic math from the extremal behavior of the microscopic math.

The major hurdle in this step concerned the length of time that the equations were modeling. Mathematicians already knew how to derive the Boltzmann equation from Newton's laws on very short timescales, but that doesn't suffice for Hilbert's program, because real-world fluids can flow for any stretch of time. With longer timescales comes more complexity: more collisions take place, and the entire history of a particle's interactions might bear on that particle's current behavior. The authors overcame this obstacle by doing careful accounting of just how much a particle's history affects its present and leveraging new mathematical techniques to argue that the cumulative effects of prior collisions remain minor.

Gluing together their long-timescale breakthrough and previous work on deriving the Euler and Navier-Stokes equations from the Boltzmann equation unifies three theories of fluid dynamics. The finding justifies taking different perspectives on fluids based on what's most useful in context because mathematically they converge on one ultimate theory describing one reality. Assuming the proof is correct, it breaks new ground in Hilbert's program. We can only hope that with just such fresh approaches, the dam will burst on Hilbert's challenges, and more physics will flow downstream.

About the Author

Jack Murtagh is a freelance math writer and puzzle creator. He writes a column on mathematical curiosities for Scientific American *and creates daily puzzles for the Morning Brew newsletter. He holds a Ph.D. in theoretical computer science from Harvard University. Follow him on X @JackPMurtagh*

Dennis Gaitsgory, Who Proved Part of Math's Grand Unified Theory, Wins Breakthrough Prize

By Manon Bischoff

The Langlands program has been described by mathematician Edward Frankel as the "grand unified theory of mathematics." Conceived by Robert Langlands in 1967, the program includes numerous conjectures that were intended to connect disparate mathematical realms: number theory and harmonic analysis. In the 1990s, a similar connection between geometry and harmonic analysis was noticed, and the geometric Langlands program was born. Decades later, in 2024, Dennis Gaitsgory of the Max Planck Institute for Mathematics in Bonn, Germany, and eight of his colleagues achieved a breakthrough. In five scientific preprint papers, consisting of nearly 1,000 pages, they proved that a large class of geometric objects is related to quantities from calculus. Gaitsgory has now been awarded the Breakthrough Prize in Mathematics, which includes a $3-million award, for this outstanding achievement.

Scientific American's German-language sister publication *Spektrum der Wissenschaft* spoke to Gaitsgory about his math career, the Langlands achievement and the prestigious Breakthrough Prize.

[*An edited transcript of the interview follows.*]

You've been working on the geometric Langlands program for 30 years. When was the moment that you realized you'd be able to prove it?

There was a very crucial step that was always a mystery. This got solved by a former graduate student of mine, [mathematician] Sam Raskin, and his graduate students in the winter of 2022. They proved that something is nonzero. After this, it was clear that we would be able to work out a proof.

How did you feel when you realized that it could really be done?

I've always perceived it as some kind of long-term project for self-entertainment. So I obviously felt happy, but it was not like a very strong emotion or anything. It wasn't a eureka moment.

The conjecture that we proved is one particular case of something much, much bigger. It has received a lot of attention because it's one well-formulated thing. But it's just one step. I was happy that this step had been done, but there's much more to do.

So there was no champagne popping? You just sat down and continued working?

There was no champagne but something similar. When [Raskin] said that he could prove this crucial part, we made a bet: if he could really do it, I promised him a bottle of scotch.

The proof is huge, almost 1,000 pages. Did you oversee everything in it?

I wrote 95 percent of it. [That was] not for a good reason but because I had an injury from skiing, and I was just lying in bed. So what else was there to do? I was watching *Star Wars* with my son and writing this thing.

Do you mean you did both at the same time?

Initially, some sections in our papers were named after Star Wars episodes, but at the end, we deleted [that element], mostly out of copyright concerns. But one paper still has a quote from Star Wars: "Fear will keep the local systems in line." It was a really good fit, because in this paper, we had to control the moduli space of local systems.

It's one thing to understand something but another to write everything down in detail. Did any problems pop up?

Of course. We had a road map, but there were still a lot of blanks to fill, many theories to be developed.

But I don't think there was a moment of actual panic. Sometimes I was not sure if one thing would require three more pages, 20 more pages or 50 more pages. There was just an uncertainty of how much more work had to be done.

Did you do all of this from your bed?

No, actually it was a cooperative process. The proof has nine co-authors: Every day I was writing to this guy and to that guy. They all have different perspectives and a slightly different kind of expertise. In some sense, it was as if I was lying in bed, and my colleagues were visiting me, so I didn't get bored. It really held my spirits up that I could talk to them by e-mail.

There are some people who go to a bar to drink; we instead just talk about math. They talk about soccer; we talk about math. It's the same thing; it's human interaction.

Speaking of human interaction, do you talk about your work with your friends and family?

No. They're not mathematicians. They can't technically understand. My wife was close by my side and knows the story and the development of the topic. She knows how these things look from the outside, but I can't describe the content [to her].

A lot of people would say that the Langlands program is one of the most complex research topics in the world. Would you agree?

The question is: What do you mean by complex? Yes, one cannot come from the street and just study this. But the same applies to what other mathematicians, such as Peter Scholze [who studies arithmetic geometry at the University of Bonn in Germany and the Max Planck Institute for Mathematics], are doing. I don't have the background to just come to a talk he is giving and understand what he says because there are lots of technical details.

It's the same here. One has to invest some effort to understand how things work, and then one should be able to understand. But that doesn't say that whatever we're doing is intrinsically more complex. I think all frontier math is equally complicated. We're all trying to push a boundary at different points.

How many people can understand the technical parts of your work?
Now the community is growing because people are studying our proof. But up until last year, apart from [my] eight co-authors, there may have been five or six people who would have the capacity to understand the technical details.

Do you wish that more people were involved in this type of research?
Yes, definitely. So far it has been a very small community: The people who pushed the boundaries were basically my former students plus Dima Arinkin [a math professor at the University of Wisconsin–Madison], who is my age. He was a close friend and collaborator for many years. So some ideas get recycled. It would be just nice to have an influx of people from the outside. They could bring in something totally new. I would be very excited to see new ideas.

What could be done to get more people interested in the geometric Langlands problem?
More lectures and workshops on that topic, I guess. There will be a master class in Copenhagen, for example, in August. And there will be a conference in Berkeley, Calif. But now our research gets more attention because our proof is out. I regularly receive e-mails, mostly from younger people.

[At the time of my interview], for example, [I am set to give] a talk to a big audience of graduate students in Graz, Austria. I will talk about the foundations of derived algebraic geometry. So the graduate students want to study these foundations, and hopefully some of them will proceed to study the geometric Langlands program. But they need derived algebraic geometry to understand this. [Editor's Note: This talk was scheduled for April 2.]

So you hope to catch the interest of young students by teaching them derived algebraic geometry. How did you become interested in the Langlands program in the first place?

It was back in the 1990s, when [Alexander] Sasha Beilinson [a mathematician now at the University of Chicago] came to Tel Aviv [University], where I was a graduate student. Beilinson gave two talks; he was at the very beginning of his own work on the subject. And I was completely captivated. I had learned about the classical Langlands program..., but before his talk, I had no idea that it could be related to geometry. It was the first time I heard about it. The objects he talked about seemed so appealing to me. It was exactly the type of mathematical object that I wanted to study. And they all came together miraculously in this. And I was like, "Wow." I had to work on that.

Does the same fascination still drive your research?

Of course things evolved. It's one thing when you're 20, another thing when you're 50. I don't know what drives me now. It's like an actual desire. It's like appetite. I want to do math. And if I can't, if I'm prevented from doing math, such as when I'm on a family vacation for a week with my kids, and I can't do math, I suffer.

Really? That happens after one week?

One week is maybe still okay. But after two weeks, I become a terrible human being.

Well, it's wonderful to find such a passion in life.

It's not really passion.

Is it maybe more like some kind of addiction?

Yes, maybe. It's more like: man needs to eat, and man needs to do math.

What are you working on now? Did you plunge into an abyss?
I am trying to generalize our work. I have several projects at different stages. There's a lot of theory to be developed, but at least we now have a program. We know what we want.

You have a new road map?
Let's say that we have the road map of desires but not a roadmap of methods like the one I [described] in 2013 [and published in 2015]. Back then, I knew exactly what needed to be proved. Now I know what I want, but I don't know how to get there.

Maybe you will get new ideas from new researchers.
That would be very nice. But I think, in some sense, it's like a Darwinian process: If the math is valuable, it will get studied. And more people will understand and get attracted. And if the math is boring, then too bad. Time will show.

About the Author

Manon Bischoff is a theoretical physicist and an editor at Spektrum der Wissenschaft, *the German-language sister publication of* Scientific American.

Abel Prize Goes to Pioneer Whose 'Math Toolbox' Can Be Used to Describe the Natural World

By Manon Bischoff

One of the landmarks of Kyoto, the home of Japanese mathematician Masaki Kashiwara, is the Kamo River. At certain points, there are stepping stones that allow residents to cross the river away from the bridges. If you take a closer look at these stones, you can see how the water forms swirls and small eddies around them. Describing this flow of a liquid is not easy. You have to solve complicated equations that have been known for centuries but still pose many mysteries today: Do the equations always have a solution? How can they be calculated? And what properties do they have? It seems that mathematicians have reached a limit with the tools of their trade. To make progress, a new toolbox is needed. Kashiwara developed such a toolbox for similarly difficult questions in the 1970s.

Kashiwara introduced proven methods from algebra into analysis–the theory underlying calculus that explores functions, limits, and other concepts–and, together with his colleagues, founded an entirely new branch of mathematics: algebraic analysis. This move led to significant advances in various fields. For example, Kashiwara succeeded in solving one of the problems posed by German mathematician David Hilbert in the early part of the 20th century, and he developed new techniques that are now used in modern physics.

Kashiwara "has proved astonishing theorems with methods no one had imagined. He has been a true mathematical visionary," read a press release from the Norwegian Academy of Science and Letters, which in March honored him with the 2025 Abel Prize–one of the highest honors in mathematics. Born near Tokyo in 1947, Kashiwara discovered his passion for mathematics at an early age through traditional Japanese puzzles known as *tsurukamezan*. These puzzles involve correctly calculating the number of cranes and turtles: Suppose x heads and y legs are visible. How many cranes and turtles are there? Kashiwara's parents didn't have much exposure to the abstract subject, but their son enjoyed solving this problem by using algebraic methods.

Here's one example: Each crane or turtle has two or four legs, respectively (y), and each has one head (x). Calculate the number of cranes (k) and turtles (s) by solving the following equations: $2k + 4s = y$ and $k + s = x$. For example, if 16 legs and five heads are visible, then there must be two cranes and three turtles.

Kashiwara realized he enjoyed generalizing such questions. He excelled in school. When he met the late mathematician Mikio Sato as one of Sato's students at the University of Tokyo, he devoted himself to this type of problem-solving. Kashiwara was in the right place at the right time. Sato and his colleagues were then developing a completely new branch of mathematics that combines two distinct fields: analysis and algebra.

Nothing Stands Still

Kashiwara worked with his mentor on differential equations. In our world, everything is in motion; nothing remains permanently still. Even a gigantic mountain range such as the Himalayas grows or shrinks over time. Such changes can be expressed mathematically with the help of derivatives. All of physics is based on equations that contain derivatives, so-called differential equations. They can be used to describe the population of living organisms, the trajectory of the moon or the flow velocity of the Kamo River.

Differential equations can be written down quickly, but they take much longer to solve. In some special cases, the solution is known. In others, however, it is not even clear whether a problem can be solved at all. One of the most important unsolved problems in mathematics revolves around the question of whether the Navier-Stokes equations, which describe the flow behavior of fluids, always have a solution. Despite centuries of research in the field of analysis, many of the most pressing problems remain unsolved.

When you're stuck on a problem, it sometimes helps to look at it from a different perspective. Often it is useful to step back and examine the problem from a distance. The exact details may become blurred, but the general structure of the topic could become visible. This approach not only helps with practical, everyday problems but also can be beneficial in mathematics.

A Japanese research group led by Sato pursued such an approach. The team wanted to examine differential equations from a different perspective. To do so, the researchers left the field of analysis and turned instead to algebra. Algebra is generally much more abstract: the focus is not necessarily the mathematical objects–in this case, the equations and their derivatives–but rather their behavior. Just as physicists study a new particle by examining its interactions with other particles, mathematicians can look at the interplay of different equations to uncover new insights. That is the idea underlying algebraic analysis.

So instead of picking out a specific differential equation and examining it in detail, Sato and his colleagues devoted themselves to an entire class of such equations. They also allowed the differential equations to move not only on a plane but also on curved surfaces–as if trying to describe a river on an oddly shaped planet. This approach may seem quite complex, but it actually opens up entirely new possibilities, allowing one to derive general properties for the class of differential equations under consideration that are not apparent for individual equations.

At the end of the 1960s, Sato organized a weekly seminar in which participants worked together to develop the concepts of the new theory. Among all the experts was Kashiwara, then a young student, who eagerly participated.

Into the Fast Lane with D-Modules

In 1970 Kashiwara began his master's thesis under Sato. His task was to develop algebraic tools for investigating objects from analysis. Then only 23 years old, Kashiwara introduced so-called *D*-modules, which make it possible to extract valuable information from differential equations. *D*-modules can be used, for example, to determine whether the solutions to equations contain "singularities"–that is, whether there are regions where they assume infinite values. The modules can also be used to calculate how many solutions the equations have.

The results of Kashiwara's master's thesis shaped the emerging field of algebraic analysis. He had written his research in Japanese, however–25 years went by before it was translated into English and thus made accessible to a wider audience.

After graduating, Kashiwara went to Kyoto University, where he continued his collaboration with Sato and earned his doctorate. In doing so, he further developed the new methods he had established in his master's thesis. "From 1970 to 1980, Kashiwara solved almost all the fundamental questions of *D*-module theory," recalled his colleague Pierre Schapira, now an emeritus professor at Sorbonne University in Paris, in a 2008 preprint paper based on a 2007 talk. After completing his doctorate, Kashiwara accepted a position at Nagoya University, conducted research for a year at the Massachusetts Institute of Technology and then returned to Japan in 1978 to accept a professorship at Kyoto University.

With the help of *D*-modules, in 1980 Kashiwara solved one of the most important problems in the field, a problem Hilbert had presented in his centenary address at the International Congress of Mathematicians in Paris in 1900. Hilbert considered 23 problems to be groundbreaking for 20th-century research; the 21st problem deals with differential equations. Hilbert wanted to know whether it would always be possible to find a differential equation whose solution possessed singularities on a given curved surface. Kashiwara was able to prove that it is indeed possible for certain types of surfaces–in those cases, a suitable differential equation can be calculated.

D-modules have led to advances in many different areas of mathematics. But they are also proving helpful in physics. In 2023 mathematician Anna-Laura Sattelberger of the Max Planck

Institute for Mathematics in the Sciences in Germany and other experts used D-modules to evaluate quantum physical "path integrals." These integrals are used to calculate which processes take place in particle accelerators when, for instance, two protons collide, creating a series of new particles. The extremely complex integrals can be viewed as solutions of differential equations, which is why the methods of algebraic analysis can help to determine their properties.

On Symmetries and Quantum Groups

Kashiwara also had a significant influence on other areas of mathematics. One of them is representation theory, which is used to describe symmetries. An object is considered symmetrical if it looks the same after certain transformations (such as rotations or reflections). For example, an equilateral triangle can be rotated by multiples of 120 degrees without changing its shape. Representation theory enables experts to calculate symmetry transformations: What happens, for example, if you combine a 270-degree rotation with a reflection along the *y*-axis? Such questions can be answered particularly well if you represent the symmetry transformations by using matrices: the combination of transformations corresponds to the multiplication of the corresponding matrices.

Suitable representations cannot be found for all types of symmetries, however. In the course of his work, Kashiwara focused extensively on continuous symmetries, known in mathematics as Lie groups. He made significant progress in investigating their representations.

He also explored discrete "quantum groups" that are not continuous. Such discrete quantum groups play an important role in quantum physics. At the microscopic level, most quantities appear only in small pieces; the world appears to be quantized at the smallest scale. To describe the symmetries of quantized quantities, Kashiwara introduced the concept of crystal bases. These bases allow quantum groups to be represented by directed networks, which offers enormous advantages. Questions of representation theory can then be answered through combinatorial considerations (arranging objects in a finite set), which are generally much simpler. These concepts have since proved their worth in both mathematics and physics.

In its Abel Prize press release, the Norwegian Academy of Science and Letters quotes its president, Annelin Eriksen, as saying, "For over 50 years Masaki Kashiwara has reshaped and deeply enriched the fields of algebraic analysis and representation theory." Kashiwara has already received numerous awards for all of this impressive research. The Abel, which honors a mathematician's lifetime achievement, marks a culmination of his accomplishments. The prize is modeled on the Nobel Prizes, which do not include mathematics, and comes with 7.5 million Norwegian kroner (approximately $760,000).

Now nearly 80 years old, Kashiwara does not seem to be thinking about retirement: he still regularly publishes new research findings and tries to enrich mathematics with new stepping stones.

About the Author

Manon Bischoff is a theoretical physicist and an editor at Spektrum der Wissenschaft, the German-language sister publication of Scientific American.

Mathematicians Solve Decades-Old Spinning Needle Puzzle

By Manon Bischoff

It is rare to read about "spectacular progress" or a "once-in-a-century" result in mathematics. That's for good reason: if a problem has not had a solution for many years, then completely new approaches and ideas are usually needed to tackle it. This is also the case with the innocent-looking "Kakeya conjecture," which relates to the question of how to rotate a needle in such a way that it takes up as little space as possible.

Experts have been racking their brains over the associated problems since 1917. But in a preprint paper posted in February, mathematician Hong Wang of New York University and her colleague Joshua Zahl of the University of British Columbia finally proved the three-dimensional version of the Kakeya conjecture. "It stands as one of the top mathematical achievements of the 21st century," said mathematician Eyal Lubetzky of N.Y.U. in a recent press release.

Suppose there is an infinitely narrow needle on a table. Now you want to rotate it 360 degrees so that the tip of the needle points once in each direction of the plane. To do this, you can hold the needle in the middle and rotate it. As it rotates, the needle then covers the surface of a circle.

But if you are clever, the needle can make its 360-degree journey while taking less space. In 1917 mathematician Sōichi Kakeya wanted to investigate the smallest area required to rotate the needle. For example, by rotating not only the outer end of the needle but also its center, you can obtain an area that corresponds to a triangle with curved sides.

Years later, mathematician Abram Besicovitch made an unexpected discovery. If you keep moving the needle back and forth like a complex parallel parking maneuver, the surface that the infinitely narrow needle covers can actually have a total area of zero.

The Dimension of an Area of Zero?

From there, experts began to wonder what dimension this "Kakeya surface" has. Usually surfaces in a plane, such as a rectangle or a circle, are two-dimensional. But there are exceptions: fractals, for example, can also have fractional dimensions, meaning they can be 1.5-dimensional, for instance.

Because the Kakeya surfaces can look very jagged, the question of dimensionality is an obvious one. In fact, it has implications for many other areas of mathematics, including harmonic analysis, which breaks down complicated mathematical curves into sums of simpler functions, and geometric measure theory.

In fact, in 1971 mathematician Roy Davies was able to prove that the Kakeya surface is always two-dimensional, even if its area vanishes. But in mathematics, people are interested in general results. The experts wanted to solve the problem in n dimensions–does a needle that is rotated along all n spatial directions always cover an n-dimensional volume? This hypothesis is now known as the Kakeya conjecture.

The three-dimensional case proved to be an extremely hard nut to crack. Over the decades, experts have been able to rule out the possibility that a rotating needle covers a volume with less than 2.5 spatial dimensions, but that was as far as they got.

Wang and Zahl were not discouraged, however, and worked their way forward step by step. Through painstaking effort, they gradually managed to eliminate all cases in which the covered volume would have a dimension of less than three.

In this way, they were finally able to prove the Kakeya conjecture in three spatial dimensions, showing that the volume covered by the needle is always three-dimensional. In the recent press release, mathematician Guido de Philippis of N.Y.U.

commented, "I am expecting that their ideas will lead to a series of exciting breakthroughs in the coming years."

About the Author

Manon Bischoff is a theoretical physicist and an editor at Spektrum der Wissenschaft, *the German-language sister publication of* Scientific American.

GLOSSARY

baryon A subatomic particle made up of quarks and subject to strong nuclear force.

biomedicine The application of biological and chemical principles to the process of understanding human health and disease with the purpose of developing new diagnostic tests and treatments.

disparity A noticeable, unfair, unequal difference between two or more things.

ecosystem A small community of interacting organisms.

empathize To understand the thoughts and feelings of another person.

eugenics The unethical practice of controlling reproduction to try to "improve" the human race.

gatekeeping Controlling access to a community, resources, or information.

genome A complete set of DNA in every cell of an organism.

hadrons A subatomic particle made up of quarks, with a baryon being one of the classifications of a hadron.

hematology A branch of medicine focused on diseases and treatment related to blood.

heuristically A mental shortcut or "rule of thumb."

hydrothermal The action of water heated underground that creates new minerals.

nephrology The study of diagnosing and treating kidney disease.

neuroscience The study of the nervous system and how the brain and nerves interact and function.

paradox Something that seems self-contradictory.

predisposition A natural tendency to behave a certain way.

quarks The fundamental building blocks of matter that form protons and neutrons, which make up an atom.

subatomic particles Tiny units of matter.

systemic Something affecting or relating to an entire organization or society.

FURTHER INFORMATION

"Celebrating Accomplishments in American STEM History." Mission: Ignite. February 24, 2022. www.missionignite.org/blogs/celebrating-accomplishments-in-american-stem-history.

Deiss, Heather. "Katherine Johnson: A Lifetime of STEM." NASA. February 24, 2020. www.nasa.gov/learning-resources/katherine-johnson-a-lifetime-of-stem/.

DNLee, "Under-Represented and Underserved: Why Minority Role Models Matter in STEM." Scientific American. April 1, 2011. www.scientificamerican.com/blog/guest-blog/under-represented-and-underserved-why-minority-role-models-matter-in-stem/.

Gibbs, Kenneth, Jr. "Beyond "The Pipeline": Reframing Science's Diversity Challenge." Scientific American. December 17, 2014. www.scientificamerican.com/blog/voices/beyond-the-pipeline-reframing-science-s-diversity-challenge/.

Gibbs, Kenneth, Jr. "Diversity in STEM: What It Is and Why It Matters." Scientific American. September 10, 2014. www.scientificamerican.com/blog/voices/diversity-in-stem-what-it-is-and-why-it-matters/.

Gomez, Laura, Lorena Galliot, Samia Bouzid, and The Lost Women of Science Initiative."Evangelina Rodríguez Led an Extraordinary Life as the Dominican Republic's First Female Doctor." Scientific American. March 13, 2025. www.scientificamerican.com/article/evangelina-rodriguez-led-an-extraordinary-life-as-the-dominican-republics/.

Strogatz, Steven. "How Calculus Was the Unsung Hero in the Fight against HIV." Scientific American. April 1, 2019. www.scientificamerican.com/article/how-calculus-was-the-unsung-hero-in-the-fight-against-hiv/.

Sutton Lewis, Carol, Luca Evans, and The Lost Women of Science Initiative. "Mildred Weeks Wells's Work on Airborne

Transmission Could Have Saved Many Lives—If the Scientific Establishment Listened." Scientific American. May 22, 2025. www.scientificamerican.com/article/a-public-health-researcher-and-her-engineer-husband-found-how-diseases-can/.

"The Untold History of Women in Science and Technology." Obama White House Archives. Accessed March 26, 2026. obamawhitehouse.archives.gov/women-in-stem.

Unger, Deborah, Natalia Sanchez Loayza, and The Lost Women of Science Initiative. "Marie Curie's Mentorship Led to Networks of Support for Female Scientists." Scientific American. April 24, 2025. www.scientificamerican.com/article/marie-curies-mentorship-led-to-networks-of-support-for-female-scientists/.

Weinstock, Maia. "Channeling Ada Lovelace: Chien-Shiung Wu, Courageous Hero of Physics." Scientific American. October 15, 2013. www.scientificamerican.com/blog/guest-blog/channeling-ada-lovelace-chien-shiung-wu-courageous-hero-of-physics/.

CITATIONS

1.1 Finding Yourself and Your Community when You Are Black in STEM by Devin Williams (February 24, 2021); 1.2 Mentorship and Sponsorship Are Crucial for Advancing Inclusion in STEM by Marlene Stewart (August 2, 2021); 1.3 How to Fix Science's Diversity Problem by Benjamin Deen (July 11, 2020); 1.4 Where Are the Black Women in STEM Leadership? by Erika Jefferson (April 23, 2019) 1.5 The Time to Dismantle the Racial Structures That Pervade Global Science Is Now by Devin Williams (June 23, 2021); 2.1 A 100-Year-Old Theory Might Explain What's Wrong with Quantum Mechanics by Tim Folger (March 16, 2026); 2.2 Physicists Trace Particles Back to the Quantum Vacuum by Clara Moskowitz (February 4, 2026); 2.3 A "Charmed" New Particle is Discovered at World's Largest Atom Smasher by Clara Moskowitz (March 17, 2026); 2.4 What Is CRISPR, and Why Is It So Important? by Michael Tabb, Andrea Gawrylewski & Jeffery DelViscio (June 22, 2021); 2.5 FDA Approves First CRISPR Gene Editing Treatment for Sickle Cell Disease by Sara Reardon (December 8, 2023); 2.6 What Does the First Pig-to-Human Lung Transplant Mean for Xenotransplantation? by Humberto Basilio (August 29, 2025) 2.7 Diagnosing Type 1 Diabetes before Symptoms Strike by Rachel Nuwer (October 14, 2025); 2.8 Cell Transplant Therapy Offers New Hope for Type 1 Diabetes by Carin Leong (December 12, 2025); 2.9 Genetic Discoveries Could Reduce Black Women's Higher Breast Cancer Death Risk by Leah Small (February 24, 2025); 2.10 Scientists Discover Brain Network That May Cause Parkinson's Disease by Allison Parshall (February 4, 2026); 2.11 Scientists Create the Smallest-Ever Moving Cell by Saugat Bolakhe (April 1, 2023); 2.12 2021 Medicine Nobel Prize Winner Explains the Importance of Sensing Touch by Tanya Lewis (October 8, 2021); 2.13 China's Giant Underground Neutrino Observatory Just Released Its First Results—And They're Promising by Jeanna Bryner (November 26, 2025); 2.14 Is It Time to Redefine Time? by Jay Bennett (February 18, 2025); 3.1 In One Life-Changing Moment, This Former Seaman Jumped from Ships to Computer Chips by Marlene Stewart (September 20, 2021); 3.2 One of the Biggest Problems in Biology Has Finally Been Solved by Tanya Lewis (October 31, 2022); 3.3 Scientists Turned 300,000 Litter Box Visits into an AI-Powered Cat Health Monitor by Deni Ellis Béchard (October 9, 2025); 3.4 Modern Rocketry Turns 100—and NASA Says the Best is Yet to Come by Lee Billings (March 18, 2026); 4.1 This Engineer, Actor and Science Communicator Is Giving Science Its Rap by Devin Williams (November 12, 2021); 4.2 New Glasses Can Transcribe Speech in Real Time by O. Rose Broderick (October 10, 2023); 5.1 3 Revolutionary Women of Mathematics by Avery Carr (March 24, 2016); 5.2 Mathematicians Crack a Fractal Conjecture on Chaos by Lyndie Chiou (December 9, 2025); 5.3 How the World's Most Famous Code Was Cracked by Jack Murtagh (October 22, 2025); 5.4 How Teen Mathematician Hannah Cairo Disproved a Major Mathematical Wave Conjecture by Emma R. Hasson (August 4, 2025); 5.5 Mathematicians Crack 125-Year-Old Problem, Unite Three Physics Theories by Jack Murtagh (April 15, 2025); 5.6 Dennis Gaitsgory, Who Proved Part of Math's Grand Unified Theory, Wins Breakthrough Prize by Manon Bischoff (April 5, 2025); 5.7 Abel Prize Goes to Pioneer Whose 'Math Toolbox' Can Be Used to Describe the Natural World by Manon Bischoff (March 26, 2025); 5.8 Mathematicians Solve Decades-Old Spinning Needle Puzzle by Manon Bischoff (April 4, 2025).

INDEX

F

G

H

I

J

L

K

M